The Challenge of Partnership in Child Protection: Practice Guide

Social Services Inspectorate

London: HMSO

First published 1995
Second impression 1995

ISBN 0 11 321825 7

Preface

Supporting families, when necessary, to bring up their children and working in partnership with parents whose circumstances may be difficult is at the heart of our Children Act. When there are concerns about the safety and protection of a child, working with family members who may be under investigation can become one of the most difficult and sensitive tasks for all agencies. My Department recognises this and wants to provide practical guidance for social workers in this field, their managers and other agencies who are involved in child protection. We have consulted widely with all agencies involved in child protection work and with families who have themselves had experience of the child protection system. The guidance draws on the best of current practice and of findings from research in this fast developing area of work. I hope it will help social workers to consider ways of ensuring both that, the well being of children is protected and that families are fully and sensitively informed about what is happening. I also want to ensure they are encouraged to be involved and to participate in the care of their children and in decisions about their future.

John Bowis OBE MP
Parliamentary Under Secretary of State *November 1994*

Advisory Group

In the chair	Wendy Rose, Assistant Chief Inspector, Department of Health
Consultant to the Project	June Thoburn, University of East Anglia
Members	Cath Adams, West Yorkshire Police Authority
	Rosemary Arkley, Social Services Inspectorate, Department of Health
	Celia Atherton, Family Rights Group
	Lynn Baxter, Social Services Department, London Borough of Lewisham
	Hilary Foord, Social Services Inspectorate, Department of Health
	Danya Glaser, Lewisham and Guys Mental Health NHS Trust
	Frank Hancock, seconded from Kent County Council to the Social Services Inspectorate
	Moira Keyes, National Society for the Prevention of Cruelty to Children
	Lesley Lord, General Practitioner and Police Surgeon, West Yorkshire Police Authority
	Julia Mitchell, Bedfordshire Probation Service and subsequently the Vane Foundation
	Peter Munro, Social Services Inspectorate, Department of Health
	Bob Perris, Education Department – North Tyneside Metropolitan Council and subsequently the Education Department South Tyneside Metropolitan Council.
	Jean Price, Southmead Health Services NHS Trust
	Damayanti Shah, Social Services Department, Bradford Metropolitan Council

Carole Smith, Social Services Department, Kirklees Metropolitan Council

David Spicer, Legal Services (Child Care), Nottinghamshire County Council

Kathleen Taylor, Community Services Division, Department of Health

Charmian Tye, South Downs Health, NHS Trust

Liz Wilson, Social Services Department, Avon County Council

Secretariat

Jim Brown, Social Services Inspectorate, Department of Health

Stella Headly, Social Services Inspectorate, Department of Health

The Department wishes to thank all the members of the advisory group who worked hard and long attending meetings of the group and commenting on successive drafts of the guide. Thanks are also extended to those who came to the users day to discuss their own experiences and give advice about the contents of the guide. Thanks are also due to the many individuals and organisations who read drafts or sections of the guide and provided helpful comments. Last but by no means least gratitude must be expressed to Rose Hutson and Sheila Sharma for typing the script.

Contents

Chapter 1
Introduction to the Guide

1.1 'Working Together Under the Children Act 1989' was published in 1991 and emphasised the need for open mindedness, the importance of focusing on the needs of the child and value of working in partnership with families during the child protection process. This guide builds on the policy laid out in 'Working Together'. Part I explores the reasons for working in partnership and the principles on which such work should be based. Part II provides practical advice on how partnership can be used to ensure the appropriate protection of children. There are wide ranging views about how and when it is appropriate and possible to work in partnership with families if there are concerns about the safety of children. There is also a diversity of opinion about what constitutes partnership and what is meant by families in this context. This guide has been prepared after a particularly wide consultation. It draws extensively on the ideas of practitioners, managers and researchers and on the views of parents and children who have had contact with child protection services.

1.2 This guidance has been produced primarily for social workers and social services departments, because of their lead responsibility in child protection work. It acknowledges the essential roles of other disciplines in child protection and the contribution they can make to working in partnership. It recognises the complexities in this area of practice and the problems requiring debate and resolution by the multi-disciplinary team of workers engaged in child protection work. It emphasises the need for teams of workers to consider the possibilities for partnership in relation to the needs of each child and the needs of each family, and it recognises that there are different models of partnership and participatory practice which may be appropriate at different times.

1.3 This guide develops ideas from the best of current practice to provide advice for elected members, managers and practitioners to encourage them to establish an environment in which partnership with families can thrive, and in which adults and children are enabled to contribute ideas about the development of services appropriate to their needs. There is still much work to be done and it is the intention that this guide stimulate new thinking and the development of improved practice amongst those facing the challenge of partnership in child protection.

1.4 In recent years the Department of Health has commissioned a programme of research projects which have examined in depth the process and outcomes of the child protection system. An overview of this research is being prepared by the Dartington Research Unit of Bristol University for publication in 1995. This guide should be read in conjunction with this overview of research.

PART I
THE PRINCIPLES OF PARTNERSHIP

Chapter 2
The Background to Working in Partnership in Child Protection

Introduction

2.1 The Children Act 1989 gives a clear lead on working in partnership. The concept of partnership and the principles of participatory practice have emerged in response to a better understanding of the needs of families and children and the unique role and importance of adult family members in the lives of children. Developments in practice and the findings of research have shaped the legislation and guidance in which the principle of partnership is now enshrined.

Why Involve Parents?

2.2 The reasons for working in partnership can be grouped under four headings:

- Effectiveness
- Families as the source of Information
- Citizens Rights
- Empowering Parents

Effectiveness

2.3 A co-operative working relationship between the helping services and families is essential if the welfare of the child is to be ensured. This co-operative relationship is more likely to be achieved if parents are encouraged to take as large a part as possible from the outset in decisions about the protection of their child and the appropriate services need to ensure that the child remains safe. Similarly children are more likely to place their trust in those who keep them fully informed, find sensitive ways of seeking their views, and pay attention to what they say when making plans for their future.

Families as a Source of Information

2.4 Family members know more about their family than any professional can possibly know. They have unique knowledge and understanding to contribute to discussions about what has and has not happened to the child and the best way to provide protection.

Citizens Rights

2.5 Family members have rights as citizens to know what is said about them, and to contribute to important decisions about their lives and those of their children. There are far reaching and very important consequences for parents as individuals and for their continuing relationship with their children if they are confirmed as abusers. The consequences for children of being registered are equally significant and have long lasting effects. The consequences of registration are such that parents and children should be given a proper opportunity to put their views to those who decide whether a child should be registered as in need of protection.

Empowering Parents

2.6 There is research and practice evidence which demonstrate that family members experience working in partnership as beneficial. The fact that they can take part in decision making helps to build up their self-esteem and encourages adults and children to feel more in control of their lives. Professional practice which reduces a family's sense of powerlessness, and helps them to feel and function more competently, is likely to improve the well being of both parents and children.

The Words we use about Partnership in Child Protection

2.7 Terms such as family involvement, participation by families, participatory practice and partnership are often used inter-changeably. It is essential that these words should be closely defined to ensure a common understanding amongst those using them. For the purpose of this publication four approaches to partnership have been defined. These are:

- providing information
- involvement
- participation
- partnership

2.8 This list could be viewed as sequential with partnership as the goal. Such an approach is too simplistic. The basic requirement at the beginning of a working relationship must be the provision of adequate information and a willingness on the part of professionals to listen without pre-judging the situation. However, thereafter relationships may fluctuate. Partnership may be possible at one point but it may subsequently cease to be a reality because of changes in a family's circumstances or because of shifting levels of trust between families and professionals. Although these activities are described as separate, it is the nature of the professional task that they overlap and merge. There is a fine line between full involvement and the early stages of participation; similarly full participation is akin to partnership.

2.9 Inevitably there will be conflicts between the views and needs of children and adults, and often also between different adults who are important in a child's life. It may be possible to work in partnership with part of a family whilst only providing information to others.

2.10 Professionals working in child protection agencies have different tasks to fulfil and are bound by different legislative restrains. Some will be aiming at partnership and others have a remit only to provide information. It is important that professionals should be aware of and understand these differences. They should cultivate an awareness of their underlying attitudes and motivation. Some techniques which facilitate involvement and partnership can, if misused, lead to the manipulation of the family or a stereotyped response.

Providing Information

2.11 Giving clear and accurate information is essential before effective consultation, involvement and partnership can take place. Such information must be readily comprehensible and useable. Even when information has been given to a family or individual it should not be assumed that it is immediately understood. If families have special communication requirements or when they are, as in most child protection cases, under considerable stress, workers need to check that important messages have been received and understood. The written word may not always be the most appropriate method of communication and other ways should be explored, for example, by video and audio recordings, and by face to face discussion to suit the needs of different children and adults.

Involvement and Participation

2.12 Family involvement and participation are closely related activities. Involvement may be predominately passive and amount to little more than receiving information, having a non-contributory presence at meetings, endorsing other people's decisions or making minor decisions. However, when involvement becomes more active and when family members are asked to contribute to discussions and decision making on key issues, they can be said to be active participants.

Partnership

2.13 The objective of any partnership between families and professionals must be the protection and welfare of the child; partnership should not be an end in itself. From the outset workers should consider the possibility of a partnership with each family based on openness, mutual trust, joint decision making and a willingness to listen to families and to capitalise on their strengths. However, words such as equality, choice and power have a limited meaning at certain points in the child protection process. There are times when professional agencies have statutory responsibilities that they have to fulfil and powers that they have to use for the benefit of the child. Local authorities are bound by law to make enquiries or to cause enquiries to be made when they believe a child in their area may be at risk of significant harm. Even when professionals try to work with as much sensitivity as possible most families see such enquiries, and any subsequent investigation, as a painful intrusion into their lives by strangers who are critical about how they look after their children. They do not see such intervention as a partnership and they may feel angry and refuse to co-operate. In such circumstances, family involvement may amount to the professionals being as open and honest as possible and keeping the family informed about their rights and about what action the professional team is taking.

2.14 Possibilities for partnership vary from family to family. Some adults are relieved to know that the ultimate power to protect the child rests with the professionals and others chafe against this use of authority. It may be possible to agree different levels of partnership with different family members. For example, partnerships may be established more easily with those who are less implicated in the abuse or those who are more consistently stable. Similarly, it will be possible to work more closely with some children than others depending on the level of their development and the experiences which they have undergone. The depth of partnerships with family members may vary as anger cools or is re-activated, or during a remission from psychiatric illness or following treatment.

2.15 There will be families who do not wish to work in partnership with the statutory agencies either because they believe they have no problem or because of their hostility towards such bodies. Even with the most resistant of families it should be possible to engage some members in the child protection process and at the very least keep them informed about what is happening and how they could participate more fully. The guiding principle for work which encourages the involvement of and partnership with families must be that the welfare of the child is of paramount importance. In most cases close partnership will offer the best benefits for the child.

Who do we mean by Families?

2.16 In this guide the words 'family member' cover birth parents, whether they are living with the child or elsewhere, step parents, partners of a parent with parental responsibility and adopting parents. They also include children and young people who are suffering or are alleged to be suffering harm, or are likely to suffer harm; their brothers and sisters who are either still living with them or have an important part to play in their lives. Also included are grandparents and previous partners of parents. The latter, although they do not have parental responsibility, may be important to the child, and may have some helpful information or support to offer without being involved in the more complex decision making.

2.17 It is not always self-evident who is a 'family member' or 'relevant carer' in each case, nor to what extent individuals should be involved in the child protection process. Parents and children should be consulted before decisions are taken about who in the family should be involved in child protection decisions. The degree and method of involvement will differ for individual family members depending on the current dynamics within the family and their past and present relationship with the child and other adults. Some members of the family may be invited to take on a role as supporter for the child or other adults, and others may be invited to contribute to discussions and decisions. It is essential that these different roles are clear to all professionals and family members involved in the process.

2.18 It may be appropriate to include, close family friends, adults with whom the child has a particularly valued and close relationship, godparents or members of religious communities who may have taken on the role played by relatives. Children or other family members with disabilities may need an advocate who is a member of the extended family or someone from a voluntary body who has worked closely with the family and whom they trust. If a child is living with long term foster parents they should also be treated as adults who are important to the child and have a contribution to make towards ensuring his or her welfare.

The Principles of Good Practice in Partnership

2.19 Some families are known to different agencies before any child protection issues arise; the child protection episode may be one event in a long term relationship. For other families intervention may be a short period of enquiry after which contact ceases, or it may be the beginning of a longer term arrangement designed to protect the child and to provide services for the family. Whatever the nature of the contact, the essential principles supporting partnership with families remain the same. The following Essential Principles have been produced with the assistance of families, carers and professional workers. They may appear self evident but it is the experience of families that professionals often discard such principles in moments of stress and pressure in order to meet the requirements of the system and the timescale set by procedures.

Fifteen essential principles for working in partnership

2.20

- TREAT ALL FAMILY MEMBERS AS YOU WOULD WISH TO BE TREATED, WITH DIGNITY AND RESPECT
- ENSURE THAT FAMILY MEMBERS KNOW THAT THE CHILD'S SAFETY AND WELFARE MUST BE GIVEN FIRST PRIORITY, but that each of them has a right to a courteous, caring and professionally competent service
- TAKE CARE NOT TO INFRINGE PRIVACY any more than is necessary to safeguard the welfare of the child
- BE CLEAR WITH YOURSELF AND WITH FAMILY MEMBERS ABOUT YOUR POWER TO INTERVENE, and the purpose of your professional involvement at each stage
- BE AWARE OF THE EFFECTS ON FAMILY MEMBERS OF THE POWER YOU HAVE AS A PROFESSIONAL, and the impact and implications of what you say and do
- RESPECT CONFIDENTIALITY of family members and your observations about them, unless they give permission for information to be passed to others or it is essential to do so to protect the child
- LISTEN TO THE CONCERNS OF THE CHILDREN AND THEIR FAMILIES, and take care to learn about their understanding, fears and wishes before arriving at your own explanations and plans
- LEARN ABOUT AND CONSIDER CHILDREN WITHIN THEIR FAMILY RELATIONSHIPS AND COMMUNITIES, including their cultural and religious contexts, and their place within their own families
- CONSIDER THE STRENGTHS AND POTENTIAL OF FAMILY MEMBERS, as well as their weaknesses, problems and limitations
- ENSURE THAT CHILDREN, FAMILIES AND OTHER CARERS KNOW THEIR RESPONSIBILITIES AND RIGHTS, including the right to services, and their right to refuse services and any consequences of doing so
- USE PLAIN, JARGON-FREE, LANGUAGE APPROPRIATE TO THE AGE AND CULTURE OF EACH PERSON. Explain unavoidable technical and professional terms
- BE OPEN AND HONEST ABOUT YOUR CONCERNS AND RESPONSIBILITIES, plans and limitations, without being defensive
- ALLOW CHILDREN AND FAMILIES TIME TO TAKE IN AND UNDERSTAND CONCERNS AND PROCESSES. A balance needs to be found between appropriate speed and the needs of people who may need extra time in which to communicate
- TAKE CARE TO DISTINGUISH BETWEEN PERSONAL FEELINGS, VALUES, PREJUDICES AND BELIEFS, AND PROFESSIONAL ROLES AND RESPONSIBILITIES, and ensure that you have good supervision to check that you are doing so
- IF A MISTAKE OR MISINTERPRETATION HAS BEEN MADE, OR YOU ARE UNABLE TO KEEP TO AN AGREEMENT, PROVIDE AN EXPLANATION. Always acknowledge the distress experienced by adults and children and do all you can to keep it to a minimum.

Options in Partnership

2.21 The opportunity for families to influence events is an essential part of participation and partnership. Professionals and families have to recognise that some aspects of child protection are not negotiable. For example, the timing of investigative interviews, the calling of a child protection conference or the appointment of a key worker following registration. However, the time of day and the place for the child protection conference can be agreed to suit the convenience of families as well as professionals, and to facilitate everyone's attendance and contribution. Similarly it should be possible to discuss who becomes the key worker so that the role is carried by someone the family can trust and who has the relevant skills and racial and cultural attributes.

2.22 If children and adults are to influence effectively what happens to their lives they must be fully informed. They need to know on what matters there can be negotiation. They must be given information in an appropriate form so that they can understand the extent, nature and relative merits of services which are available. Equally, it is essential that they are clear about their responsibilities and commitments if they make certain decisions.

2.23 Professionals undermine their working relationship with families if they are unclear or equivocal about the extent to which options are available. Families may express a preference for a particular type of service which is not available and it is important that workers are honest about the limitations of services. It may be necessary to re-negotiate agreements, when new information comes to light or family circumstances change, so that arrangements can be adjusted to ensure the appropriate protection of the child. Professionals must be explicit about any new or changed expectations which they have about the care of the child, and they must be equally clear with adults and young people about any adjustments to the services provided for the family.

The Changing Nature of Partnership

2.24 Because the role of an individual carer has been defined in a particular way at a certain time, it does not of necessity follow that it cannot change or develop. Relationships within families, and between families and professionals, fluctuate and re-negotiation is part of protection. Some individuals may be considered unfit to make decisions at particular times or about certain issues. For example, this may be because they deny that abuse has taken place or because they disclaim any responsibility for what has happened. It will be inappropriate to involve some people because of illness, current mental instability, protracted absence or because they are assessed as being dangerous to the child. This does not rule out their involvement in other ways and their participation in decision making at other times. In due course they may be able to work in partnership with professional agencies for the benefit of the child. The child or children may have views to contribute about their vulnerability at different times and how their safety can be increased. Well-informed decisions, based on careful discussion, observation and evaluation of each situation, have to be made about when partnership is a possibility and when too much emphasis on working in partnership may be detrimental to the child. Although it is good practice to recognise the needs of individual adults in the family, and make appropriate arrangements to provide relevant services, the needs of the adults should not outweigh those of the child. The objective of partnership with families during the child protection process is to ensure the welfare of the child and efforts to work in partnership should not put the child at risk.

Involving and Empowering Children in Child Protection Work

Principles which support work with children

2.25 Children have a right to be involved in decisions which affect their lives and to express their wishes and feelings about their future. Deciding upon the level and nature of their involvement and participation in the child protection process provides one of the most demanding challenges for professionals. Decisions have to be made about each individual in relation to her or his own needs and abilities, and each child's wish to be involved in decision making.

2.26 Work of this nature needs careful preparation and planning by all those undertaking it. This includes the child's key worker, the chairs of child protection conferences and all the other workers who attend conferences and meetings at which young people may be present. Children, like adults, will need careful preparation and support throughout their involvement in the process. There is an important role for ACPCs and managers in all agencies with child protection responsibilities to provide leadership, guidance and training in work with children.

2.27 The key principles on which to base work with children are found in the Children Act 1989. Applied in practice these principles represent a significant opportunity for professionals to involve children in decisions which affect their lives. The involvement of children as contributors in the child protection process which is primarily concerned with communication between adults and in which there is a diverse range of players, many of whom have different and conflicting objectives, raises particularly complex issues. The extent to which a child participates in the process and the manner in which she or he is enabled to do so depends upon a variety of considerations. For example, the child's age and understanding, cognitive development, cultural and ethnic background, personality, and personal preference have to be taken into account. It is essential that professionals should find the most appropriate balance between enabling children to be involved whilst at the same time protecting them from exposure to stresses and conflicts inconsistent with their welfare. They will be capable of different levels of involvement and participation at different times. The ability of children to benefit from participating in the child protection process will usually increase with age and understanding but will also depend on external factors such as the degree of distress and pressure from which they are suffering at a particular time.

Building up a Working Relationship with the Child

2.28 All professionals engaging in work with children will need special skills to enable them to relate to children. They must also have an understanding of children's development and how they function when distressed. They will require sufficient time to exercise their skills and work at the individual child's pace. In order to encourage children and young people to participate as much as possible in decisions about their lives, professionals should consider what resources facilitate effective communication, for example, the availability of appropriate services for children with different intellectual abilities and special needs. There will also be a need for interpreters with training in child protection for children whose first language is not English.

2.29 At first it may only be possible to engage with children at the level of ensuring that they are given all appropriate information. This may be done verbally, in writing and in other forms that they can comprehend easily. Giving information should not be a professional monologue but rather a dialogue with the child using words and phrases appropriate to her or his understanding, and encouraging the child to ask questions, express fears and contribute ideas and wishes. Thus involvement becomes consultation bordering on participation and, as trust and understanding are established, the basis is laid for closer working with the child. It is important that the responsibility of the professionals to seek the views of the child should not be distorted by an over-simplified reliance on a child's wishes. The challenge for professionals is to strive for the most appropriate balance between the child's views, the parents' views and responsibilities and the professionals' responsibility to make appropriate and informed decisions.

Establishing a Child's Wishes and Feelings

2.30 Establishing a child's wishes and feelings is a first step towards enabling their participation. Building up rapport with a child cannot be hurried and there are no short cuts. For most children parents and carers will be involved in this process but it will also be necessary for children to be seen on their own. In all cases children will have their own perception of the situation, and in some cases there will be conflict between the child's view and that of parents or carers.

2.31 The purpose of talking to the child is to ensure that the child has an understanding of the present situation, what has happened in the past and what is likely to happen if certain decisions are made. It is important that professionals are honest in conveying to children the powers and responsibilities they have. For example, they must not promise to keep a child's secrets about the abuse she or he has suffered. A child centred approach and a willingness to enter into dialogue conducted at the child's pace is essential. This can be achieved by the giving of clear comprehensible information, by open or hypothetical questions, by the presentation of a limited number of options and by careful attention to the child's messages. Care must be taken not to give the child the impression that she or he alone carries the responsibility for decisions, but rather that professionals take decisions bearing in mind the child's expressed views. It is important that the professionals use methods of communication appropriate to the child's abilities. Some children will find verbal communication difficult or impossible and it will be necessary to help them express their feelings and thoughts in other ways, such as play, drawing and painting.

Understanding the Child's Responses

2.32 There are difficulties for professionals in gauging how informed a response each child is able to make, in particular, to what extent the child is able to comprehend and predict the likely long term consequences and outcomes if her or his wishes are fulfilled. Children do not think easily in terms of their own long term development and psychological well being. It is difficult for them to imagine what it would be like to live away from those they know and those who have always cared for them. They have pre-conceived notions about alternative care which are often ill-informed being based on information gleaned from the media or from descriptions by those using removal from home as a threat. Most children tend to express wishes for the best and ideal rather than the least detrimental alternative .

2.33 Because of their attachment needs, and regardless of the nature of abuse and harm which they have experienced at the hands of parents or carers, the majority of children do not wish to be separated from their primary carers. Their wish is for the maltreatment to stop and the blame to diminish. Other factors underlying their wish to remain with primary carers include loyalty and feelings of responsibility towards the adults. Such loyalties, as well as other experiences in a child's life, may mean that she or he states different wishes at different times. Their feelings towards carers are often mixed and it should not be assumed that there is no love for an abusing adult. Children, like persons of any age, experience a range of conflicting feelings such as love and hate, anger and longing, sadness and relief, and particularly confusion, anxiety and fear. Professionals must remain sensitive to these conflicting emotions and the reasons for them.

Taking Account of the Child's Wishes

2.34 There is a professional responsibility to ensure that the child's wishes and views are accurately represented to those making decisions, and the child should be helped to understand this process and the other factors that have to be taken into consideration when decisions are made. It must be made clear to the child who will represent her or his views, how they will be communicated, and who will make decisions. Children need to know in what way they have influenced decisions and they should always be kept fully informed about decisions taken about their lives and their future.

The attendance of children at child protection conferences, reviews and other meetings

2.35 It is impossible to set down absolute criteria about the attendance of children and young people at meetings. The first consideration is the child's capacity to benefit from the attendance; it is never acceptable to encourage the child's presence at any meeting if the experience will be detrimental to the individual. Each young person's particular situation will have to be considered and this may change over time. The advantages and disadvantages of their attendance should be evaluated with them by professionals whom they trust. When it is agreed that a child should attend a meeting it is important to consider what attendance means in each situation. Some children will wish to be present just to hear what is said and some will wish to contribute. The role of the person chairing the meeting is crucial in enabling the child to have a positive experience which is not damaging in any way, and which empowers her or him to contribute appropriately to discussion and decision making. The person chairing the conference will need to prepare for the presence of a child and will need to alert all other professionals to the sensitivities inherent to the situation.

Representation of Children and Young People's Views and Wishes at Meetings

2.36 Not all children may wish or be able to attend child protection meetings, but there are many ways in which they may present their views on these occasions. They may wish to make audio or videotapes or they may draw a picture, write a letter or compose a poem to represent their views.

2.37 Children like to think that they are 'special' and that someone will be responsible for giving their point of view independently of others. One way of managing this is for each child to be presented by their own worker. Where resources do not allow this, a child will need reassurance that her/his views will be taken into account and due time given to their consideration. Workers must be clear in their own minds when they are representing the child and when they are carrying out other roles. The person speaking on behalf of the child must ensure that she or he has a clear understanding of the child's views and that statements on behalf of the child are born out of direct and specific discussion. The child should know what will be said on her or his behalf at the meeting, as well as what other information is likely to be shared and who will hear it. Professionals need to be clear about the difference between the child's views and wishes, and decisions and recommendations made in the child's best interests. Both should have a proper and discrete place during discussion.

Dealing with Confidential Material

2.38 Some children will wish to attend meetings when professionals think that their attendance is inappropriate. There may be occasions when parents and carers or professionals do not wish children to attend all or any of the meeting for fear of what they may hear. Some professionals have considerable reservations about the involvement of both children and carers at meetings on the grounds of confidentiality. It is essential that professionals, parents and other carers are given the opportunity to express their doubts. Sometimes it may be necessary to negotiate an arrangement that enables them to share relevant confidential material without the presence of the child or young person. In addition to confidentiality agreements amongst professionals, it is important to be aware of agreements which have been made with each child, and each family member, about confidential material. If, for reasons of confidentiality or because of conflicts and stresses within the group, it is decided that it would be detrimental for the young person to attend a meeting, then reasons should be given for this decision in a form suitable to her or his understanding. Every effort should be made to represent the child's views accurately and provide feedback on the discussion and reasons for decisions made.

Attendance by Young Children

2.39 Age is a helpful factor in deciding which children and young people attend meetings. It is unlikely that children under ten years old will gain from attending child protection meetings. Their contribution will be greatly influenced by the presence of unfamiliar people. They will find it difficult to follow the proceedings or understand the language used. They will be looking to parents and carers, if they are present, for cues and prompts and permission to speak. They will find it difficult to put into context any statement about the concerns that professionals have, and they may be upset if they perceive that the adults who are important to them are being admonished.

Factors Influencing Decisions about the Attendance of Older Children

2.40 Even older children, who may be superficially more able to deal with the situation, will probably experience mixed and confused feelings if they attend child protection meetings. In many child protection matters children have acutely divided loyalties and because of this they will find attendance a difficult experience. This is an important factor in deciding if the child should attend. It is also important for professionals to be aware of the potential for increased difficulties in family relationships in the aftermath of meetings if issues are aired in such a public forum. It is particularly damaging if issues are aired for the first time in such a forum.

2.41 Children do not generally enjoy hearing unfavourable reports about themselves read out in public, even if they are well aware of their contents and have contributed to their preparation. If information is likely to be distressing, it will be essential for the professional worker who is closest to the child to consider whether attendance at the meeting might be detrimental. This is an issue on which the child is likely to have her or his own view.

2.42 Different child protection meetings are set up for different purposes. Initial child protection conferences and reviews are held not only for the exchange of information but also to provide the opportunity for professionals and families to analyse and weigh up the level of risk to the child and to make recommendations. It is not necessarily in the best interests of all children to witness this discussion. It is in the interests of the child that there are optimal conditions for professionals to discuss their concerns freely. In the most sensitive cases some professionals will not feel able to express their concern openly in the presence of the child, especially when talking about poor prognosis for the future. If it is decided that it would be detrimental for the child to attend throughout the conference it may be appropriate to invite her or him to join in for part of the meeting to represent her or his views, or to hear what decisions and future plans have been made.

2.43 Decisions about a child's attendance at a child protection conference should also be influenced by the likelihood of any criminal proceedings. Legal advice should be sought on whether or not a child's attendance, during which she or he may hear or be informed of the views of other people, could ultimately be challenged by the defence and possibly be ruled as inadmissible. In such cases other arrangements for involving the child in the process should be considered.

Preparation for Attendance

2.44 It is essential that children and young people should be prepared for attendance at child protection conferences and reviews. Every effort should be made to ensure that it is a positive experience for them. They need to have a clear understanding of the purpose of the meeting, how their views will be taken into account and the names and role of each person present. They will be empowered by having information about how the meeting will be conducted. For example, they should be given information about the content and agenda of the meeting, the layout of the room and where people will sit. It will be helpful for a child to see the room in which a conference or review is to be held and, if available, a video tape of a simulated meeting.

2.45 Every young person attending a child protection meeting should meet the person chairing the meeting in advance. This person plays a key role in ensuring that the child understands the main issues being discussed and also gives the child appropriate explanations of the process as the meeting progresses. The child's supporter can assist by asking for further explanation or encouraging the child to do so.

2.46 Children may wish to rehearse what they want to say at such a meeting. They should always be prepared for the kind of things that will be said about themselves and their parents. It is never appropriate for a child to be asked in a formal meeting to confront their adult carers or decide between them. The worker attending the meeting with the child should agree with her or him beforehand how any such situations should be handled if they arise.

The Child or Young Person at the Conference

2.47 Most meetings are complex and it may be necessary at times to adjourn to ensure that the child understands specific issues. Restricting dialogue to simple direct questions and answers does not give the child the opportunity to understand all of the issues and alternatives. People chairing conferences have a role in creating opportunities for the child to make a contribution and to assimilate information. The essential task of the person chairing the conference is to ensure that a child protection meeting fulfils its primary task of ensuring that the child is adequately protected whilst at the same time meeting the needs of the child to express her/his views and wishes.

2.48 Children need to be re-assured that adults are trying to understand their messages, and they need to be given encouragement when they speak and when they use other forms of communication. It should be confirmed to them that people have taken note of their feelings and ideas. For example, the person chairing the conference can summarise the main points and seek affirmation from the child that they are being fairly represented. The presence of children in meetings requires an investment of staff time and may prolong discussions. However, such an approach is important if the child's presence is to be a positive and useful experience.

2.49 Some children, even with a great deal of help, will find if difficult to speak in front of a group of adults, especially when they are unsure about the relationships between them. This should not of itself preclude them from attending and listening or receiving an interpretation of the dialogue. Fine decisions have to be made about what will be most beneficial for each child.

Information and Explanation about Decisions

2.50 Children should receive information about decisions and plans agreed at child protection meetings. Written records, in age-appropriate language, and their own first language, should be provided for them after meetings. Children with disabilities will need information, in braille, or on videos or audiotape. Many children may find that videos and audiotapes are more readily comprehensible and provide a better long term record for them.

2.51 It is important that there is no delay in informing children about decisions. The way in which children are informed should be agreed at the meeting and incorporated in the plan for future activity. The different agencies, parents and carers should work together to ensure that there is no conflicting or biased presentation of the decisions. Children should be given opportunities to question the reasons for decisions and should be left in no doubt that the matter can be discussed further at any time.

Children who give Evidence in Criminal Proceedings

2.52 Children who may be involved as witnesses in criminal proceedings require special attention and support. Involvement in the adult world of court processes can be traumatic for most young people and for some it can be actively harmful. Careful decisions, drawing on expert advice, have to be made about whether a child or young person should act as a witness in a criminal trial. Children and young people will have their own views about appearing in court and these must be sought and listened to. Children and young people must be clearly and explicitly advised on how the trial process works and what will be expected of them.

2.53 If it is agreed by all the professionals concerned with a case, by the child and by the adult carers that a child should act as a witness she or he will require continuing support from professionals and adult carers, and also preparation and support in relation to the court appearance. Care must be taken not to undermine the child in this role by giving the kind of support or therapy which could be interpreted in court as coaching by an examining lawyer. In some instances a child's need for therapy may be such that priority should be given to this course of action rather than the pursuit of the prosecution. This is a complex decision and can only be reached after full discussion between the agencies with statutory responsibilities, consultation with the child and relevant adult carers, and expert advice.

Information for Children and Young People

2.54 All children grow increasingly curious about their past and that of their family. Normally this need is met by families in conversation using photographs and other memorabilia. For children who have been involved in the child protection process, and particularly if changes in family structures and membership follow, there are painful and usually perplexing losses. Social workers should be proactive in initiating the keeping of records about the significant events and decisions in the child's life, and particularly how the decisions were reached. These should be regularly updated and shared with the child throughout her or his developing years.

The Importance of Race, Culture and Language in Partnership

"Abuse is not condoned by any racial group. We should not seek excuses for abuse. Children need to be protected. To work effectively and assess whether abuse has taken place we need to understand the context"—'Race and Child Protection—A Code of Practice—Race Equality Unit 1991'

Sensitivity to Ethnic and Cultural Issues

2.55 The key principles for good practice and partnership with families in child protection are universal. Children are abused in all cultures and all children have a right to be protected. Practitioners should be aware of, and sensitive to, differing family patterns, lifestyles and child rearing patterns. All professionals need to be aware of the power differentials which exist between workers and families from different cultural, ethnic and racial groupings.

2.56 In order to achieve successful partnerships with families in child protection work, professionals must give special consideration to the different cultural, ethnic and racial origins of families and their different religious beliefs and languages. The many different ethnic and cultural variations in our society require all professionals to develop a personal and organisational commitment to equality and to meeting the needs of families and children as well as understanding the effects of racial discrimination, and cultural misunderstanding or misinterpretation.

2.57 There are within society wide ranging views about what constitutes child abuse. Different ethnic and cultural groups will be influenced in their views and responses by their own religious beliefs and cultural traditions as well as their values and attitudes to family and community life. It is essential that practitioners should have a proper understanding of these influences and how they are likely to affect families involved in the child protection process. They must avoid stereotyped responses to individuals and to different groups. Also, they should have knowledge and understanding of the strengths and support systems available within ethnic groups and communities which can facilitate closer working with families and ultimately partnership.

2.58 It is important that whilst striving to be ethnically sensitive professionals must always maintain their focus on the needs of the child, the importance of making an informed and systematic assessment of her or his safety and the ability of the family to provide appropriate care. There are dangers in an over reliance on cultural explanations of child abuse, and of re-inforcing common myths and stereotypes of black and ethnic minority families, which may distort an assessment of a family's strengths and weaknesses and the potential or actual harm to a child.

The Provision of Appropriate Services in a Multi-Cultural Society

2.59 As a beginning the services for minority ethnic and black families must be accessible. It is essential that information about the child protection process is available in the language of the family and in a form that they can readily comprehend. Older children and other family members should not be asked to act as interpreters, except in brief contacts. Careful attention must be given to the choice of interpreters including consideration of their skills, their understanding of child abuse and their wider links within their local community.

2.60 Like all children those from ethnic minority and black groups are usually best protected in their own home and community. It is important that practitioners should ask families about their life style, child rearing and cultural patterns, and their expectations of service. By acknowledging the importance of a family's own traditions, and by recognising and building on their strengths partnership becomes a possibility. In order to move towards and sustain a partnership, it is essential that practitioners remain sensitive to the ethnicity of the child and family throughout the child protection process from referral, through investigation and assessment, at the child protection conference and during the implementation of any protection plan. The local area child protection committee, and its constituent agencies, should support practitioners by establishing a child protection system which meets the needs of different ethnic groups, and by ensuring that practitioners and managers receive appropriate training.

Chapter 3
The Organisational Framework for Working in Partnership in Child Protection

Introduction

3.1 It is essential to consider the organisational context in which partnership in child protection takes place. Those endeavouring to work in partnership with families are more likely to succeed if the system requires, values, supports, monitors and rewards participatory practice. Such a system will ensure that family support and child protection services are sensitive to the needs of all families, including those in which there are disabled children and adults and those families which have special requirements because of their race, culture or religion. This chapter looks at the roles and tasks of the area child protection committee, senior and middle managers, and elected local authority members.

The Work of Area Child Protection Committees

3.2 Area child protection committees (ACPCs) have responsibility for the implementation of Working Together Under the Children Act 1989, and the task of ensuring that local child protection procedures encourage partnership with families. In order to avoid contradictory practice and unhelpful diversity amongst agencies, the ACPC should give a clear lead about how partnership with families should be developed to ensure a high standard of protection for children in the area. The ACPC policy on partnership should be designed to meet local needs and should be actively promoted by all agencies represented on the ACPC. When establishing their policy ACPCs should model the style of participatory practice which they expect from their members and by consulting with the local community about the development and delivery of child protection services.

Family Participation in Planning Services

3.3 Many family members, both adults and children, have relevant advice to contribute when child protection services are being planned. Their ideas should be actively sought. Routine feedback collected systematically from users will enable members of the ACPC to judge the success of their policies and deal with any difficulties in relation to inter-agency procedures and practice. Such is the vulnerability of those against whom allegations of abuse have been made that they may not feel able to complain personally about the system. It is important that the ACPC should work closely with local user groups and voluntary organisations so that families have a source of support and can turn to an organisation which will, if necessary, speak on their behalf.

Collecting Information about Family Participation

3.4 In order to inform its policy on partnership the ACPC should gather systematically information about the frequency and nature of involvement by adults and children in all the stages of the child protection process. Some ACPCs have made considerable improvements in their services by distributing simple questionnaires to families to solicit their views about how services should be developed. Basic information about the representation of different groups at child protection conferences can be illuminating. For example, details about parental attendances, the presence of children, those attending from minority groups, adults and children with disabilities, can indicate trends in practice. These can be explored further by means of short dipstick exercises.

ACPC Annual Reports

3.5 Every ACPC is required to produce an annual report which can be a vehicle for publicising its policy on partnership. Information and statistics about participation in the process can be included in these reports as can details about consultations with and complaints from those who have used the services. The report should also contain details of special initiatives which encourage partnership, and information about specific guidance or training material which has been produced.

Special Initiatives

3.6 Initiatives to enhance partnerships may be aimed at professionals and/or at families. Ideally initiatives for each of these groups should be complementary. Both must contain similar messages which are readily comprehensible and above all useable. For families this advice should be produced in the major languages of the local community, and in a format that is easily accessible to people with communication difficulties.

Complaints and Representation

3.7 One of the key components of partnership with families under the Children Act 1989 is access to complaints and representation procedures. Families need procedures which can be activated easily and resolve difficulties speedily. They should be made aware of the existence of complaints procedures at the time of their first contact with the child protection system and should be reminded subsequently of their right to complain and how they can do this.

3.8 It is essential that professionals endeavouring to work in partnership are clear about what complaints procedures cover and how they are invoked. By being clear themselves they will be able to explain to families how they can use these procedures. To assist families the ACPCs should provide easily comprehensible information in appropriate formats about local complaints procedures. Children as well as adults may have cause for complaint and professionals should ensure that children are able to use the procedures.

The Responsibility of Managers

3.9 Managers in all agencies have a key role in the development of participatory practice and partnership with families. Strong leadership by managers at all levels is essential if partnership is to work for the benefit of children and they are not to be put at risk by an imprecise and unclear understanding of partnership with families. Managers must accept responsibility for defining policies in relationship to partnership and ensuring standards of good practice which engage parents in the process and at the same time safeguard the interests of children.

An Overall Child Care Strategy

3.10 The participation of families in the child protection process has to be considered in the context of an authority's child care strategy; policies and standards should be consistent throughout an agency's child care work. However, there are particular challenges for child protection workers. Managers need to be aware of the complexities of working with families following allegations of abuse and must ensure that the special features of this work are spelt out clearly in policy and practice guidance.

The Work of Managers with Other Agencies

3.11 Managers have an important responsibility for negotiating good working relationships with other agencies. Whilst acknowledging and respecting the different roles of agencies, all managers should identify and encourage common understanding and joint approaches to involvement, participation and partnership with families. Senior managers, who sit on the ACPC, should use this forum to negotiate policies and standards acceptable to all agencies. Middle managers and local team leaders have an equally important task negotiating with their local counterparts in other organisations to ensure that policies are implemented consistently across all agencies.

The Appropriate Use of Resources

3.12 An important role for all managers is to ensure that the child protection system is used appropriately. Most families find their passage through the child protection system stigmatising and stressful. The effects of such trauma can be long lasting and detrimental to relationships between adults and children and between families and professionals. Properly integrated services, which are planned to encourage the involvement of families as early and as fully as possible in all decisions, should ensure that families receive services appropriate to their needs without being filtered into the child protection system as the only gateway to the provision of multi-agency services. In order to ensure the proper use of the child protection system, managers should monitor how it works and ensure that there are alternative ways of families gaining access to an appropriate range of supportive services

Leadership to Change Attitudes and Practices

3.13 Partnership with families during the child protection process requires vigorous leadership by managers at all levels to change unhelpful attitudes and influence the redistribution of resources. The resources needed to support such changes include:

- a trained work force equipped to undertake a range of tasks. For example, these include face to face work with parents and with children, supervision of staff working towards partnership, the chairing of child protection conferences at which families are present
- a training programme specifically directed at enabling all staff to acquire the appropriate skills and understanding on which successful partnership with parents is dependent
- readily available information about the child protection system which is clear and concise and can be obtained early by families through professionals and in public places
- receptionists who provide a courteous welcome and enable families to feel at ease
- a sufficient number of interview rooms in which families can feel comfortable and relaxed
- an efficient administrative system with personnel who understand the importance of facilitating family participation
- a referral system which facilitates easy self referral and re-referral
- an intake and follow-up system which is sensitive to the needs of families who find it stressful and inhibiting to be interviewed and visited by a succession of professionals
- an allocation system in which there is sufficient flexibility to allow for the appropriate matching of professionals with families, change of workers when necessary, and on occasions the involvement of more than one worker to meet the needs of individuals
- a policy on recording which facilitates partnership with families through easy access to records, family involvement in recording and the use of written agreements
- readily available financial assistance which encourages the involvement of parents in meetings and discussions

- a system of support for families which helps them take part as fully as possible in child protection conferences and other meetings. Local voluntary organisations or self-help groups can provide this kind of service or social services departments may wish to set up an internal support service
- provision of good quality supervision and consultation for staff working in partnership with families
- a system which ensures that child care workers have access to advice from colleagues who work with people who have special needs and requirements, that the skills of such staff are used to facilitate communication and partnership with adults and children
- a means of providing quickly the expert guidance which is required in relation to particularly difficult or complex situations. For example, the expert psychiatric advice needed during an assessment commissioned to consider the possibilities for working in partnership with a parent or carer who has a history of mental disability.

3.14 It is important that managers should find ways of consulting parents and children, who are past or present recipients of child protection services, about the models of service delivery which they find most helpful and which offer the best protection for children. It is essential that this consultation should include people with disabilities and those whose first language is not English.

The Responsibility of Elected Members

The Role of Elected Members

3.15 Families and children involved in the child protection system are of necessity recipients of services delivered by the social services department. Elected members are accountable for the provision of these services and for their quality. They should be aware of relevant legislation and of current good practice, and they should understand the reasons why it is important to work closely with families and encourage them to participate in meetings and decision making. Elected members have a key role in sanctioning the necessary changes in policy and in agreeing any redistribution of resources to support new practices and projects. Their agreement and support are also necessary if resources are to be made available across agency and departmental boundaries as required under Section 27 of the Children Act 1989, and if policies and strategies developed by the ACPC are to be endorsed and become effective.

Promoting Family Participation and Partnership

3.16 Local authority members can play an important role in developing services which are sensitive to the needs of families and encourage partnership. They can:

- encourage the local authority to develop strategies and policies that support the involvement of and partnership with families

- ask for regular reports on the progress of these policies within the local authority
- ask for reports on the work of the ACPC including information on the extent and nature of participatory practice, details about complaints, and about methods of consulting those who receive multi-agency child protection services
- ensure that the Annual Report of the ACPC is discussed in all the relevant committees of the local authority
- ensure that adults and young people who receive child protection services are consulted about their effectiveness and how they could be improved
- ensure that the provision of child protection services is evaluated, and that specific attention is given to examining the implementation of policies which cover participatory practice and partnership
- consider the provision of grants and other ways of promoting local support groups and self help groups for those enaged in the child protection process

3.17 The role of elected members is crucial to the development of partnership with families. They can give positive encouragement to senior and middle managers in social services departments, and through their support of these staff they can influence positively the work of the other agencies represented on the ACPC.

PART II
PARTNERSHIP IN PRACTICE

Introduction to Part II

Part II of this guide provides advice for practitioners and their immediate managers on working in partnership with families at the different stages of the child protection process. Working Together under the Children Act 1989 outlines six stages which are used here because they are familiar to practitioners.

- Referral and recognition
- Immediate protection and planning the investigation
- Investigation and initial assessment
- Child protection conference and decision making about the need for registration
- Comprehensive assessment and planning
- Implementation, review, and when appropriate de-registration

These stages in the child protection process are not completely separate as they often merge and overlap. However, for ease of reference each activity is dealt with in a separate chapter each of which highlights the opportunities for co-operation and partnership.

Chapter 4
Referral and Recognition

Introduction

4.1 The basis for partnership with families is established at the time of recognition and referral. Much depends on the willingness of practitioners to work from the outset in a way that facilitates the involvement of and partnership with adults and children.

4.2 Referrals may arise in a number of ways. For example:

- self referral
- referral by a family member
- referral by a friend, a neighbour or an anonymous person
- referral by a professional

Self-Referral

4.3 Self-referrals are made by adults who wish to talk about their needs and concerns which may or may not be expressed in terms of child protection. Others will wish to talk about suspicions and fears that abuse is being perpetrated by a partner. Children also seek help. Self-referral is likely to be a painful experience and adults and children will have doubts and fears about what will happen as a result of their action, and they may have some suspicion of and hostility towards those empowered to take action. Some families will have had earlier contact with the social services department and this will have set the scene for this new referral. The first interview is crucial, as it sets a pattern for the future working relationship.

4.4 All those making self-referrals should be treated with respect and courtesy. They should be given every opportunity to explain their needs as clearly as possible. It is important that they are encouraged to be honest and are made aware that the professional is listening carefully with an open mind before taking any action.

4.5 In the majority of cases there will be no need for immediate action to protect the child and no need for legal action to remove the child from home, but the current safety of the child should be discussed and assessed. When there is a need for legal action to protect the child this should not be avoided for the sake of preserving the possibilities for working in partnership in the future. There should be discussion with the referrer about what she or he sees as any specific source of harm to the child and what could be done to alleviate the situation.

4.6 Professionals should be honest with both adults and young people about the extent of their legal responsibilities and the procedures that they have to follow. Those making referrals should be made aware that the worker to whom they are talking is likely to discuss the referral with a supervisor or manager before there is a final decision on future action. They must be given a clear outline and explanation of any subsequent action that may be necessary. If young people make referrals personally it is important to discuss with them how non-abusing parents can become involved.

4.7 At this time a careful judgement should be made about whether the present danger, or likelihood of harm to the child, requires further enquiries to be made or whether it would suffice to offer assistance under Section 17 of the Children Act 1989. The Department of Health provides leaflets for parents and children about Part III of the Children Act 1989 which should be made available to families at this time. If it becomes obvious that further enquiries under child protection procedures are needed, but child protection issues were not the original concern of the referrer, this is likely to be a distressing development to the person making the referral and she or he may wish to withdraw. The impossibility of this must be explained and every effort should be made to engage the family as positively as possible in the further work.

4.8 Ideally, if it is decided to follow the child protection procedures and make further enquiries under Section 47 of the Children Act 1989 appropriate family members, including the person making the referral, should be informed of the decision. When it is decided that this is necessary, the reasons for this action and the specific responsibilities of the professionals undertaking this work must be clearly explained to the family. Also families should be made aware that a strategy discussion will take place to plan further work. This should be done unless telling them would place the child at risk.

Referral by a Family Member

4.9 People make referrals about other members of their families for a variety of reasons ranging from genuine concern to malicious intent. The sensitive handling of such referrals is crucial because the safety of the child may be at stake. Also the relationship between the family and the professionals in the future may be jeopardised if the seeds of mistrust are sown at this stage. Whenever possible family members making allegations should be persuaded to give professionals permission to attribute the allegations when discussing them with those who have responsibility for the welfare of the child.

4.10 Referrals from family members should always be taken seriously. As with all referrals it is important to make an evaluation of the information received and an assessment of the child's immediate safety. Some family members may choose to make a child protection referral recognising that this will activate a particularly responsive system. All people making referrals need some feedback about action taken in response to their allegations. Family members are no exception, and, it is particularly important to safeguard confidential information in this situation.

Referral by a Friend, Neighbour or an Anonymous Person

4.11 It is sometimes difficult for families to understand why allegations made by friends and neighbours must be followed up, especially if they see this intervention as vindictive and intrusive. It is important to help them understand that agencies with statutory responsibilities have to take all such referrals seriously because of possible risks to the child. Anonymous referrals must be treated seriously and care should be taken whenever possible not to expose the caller to the possibility of identification.

Referral by a Professional Worker in the Child Protection Network

4.12 Before making a referral to an agency with the statutory responsibility to make further enquiries into the possibility of child abuse other professionals should have given careful consideration to the grounds for such a referral, and as appropriate discussed the need for it with colleagues in the same discipline and with the agencies with statutory responsibilities. Their concern having reached a critical threshold they will wish to make a formal referral. Preliminary discussions with the social services department may facilitate the mobilisation of appropriate services without the need for a child protection referral, but in some instances such will be the accumulated concern that it becomes clear that further enquiries are necessary.

4.13 It is good practice for the need for referral to be discussed with the family. If this has not been done, it is important that those receiving the referral should discuss with the referrer the importance of being able to talk as openly as possible with the family about the source and the nature of the allegation or concern. It will be necessary to agree with the referring professional what information can be shared with the family. This approach may be hard for some people to accept as they may believe that their action will be seen by the family as a betrayal and that this will undermine their previously good relationship. However, honesty is important if the child protection concerns are to be explored thoroughly, and if the family is to trust professionals sufficiently so that they can be involved in any decision making and planning about the child.

4.14 There may be a reluctance by professionals to go down this path because of fears for their own safety or that of the child. Such fears have to be taken seriously and evaluated against what is known about a family. It may be necessary to consider arrangements for ensuring the safety of workers. It will always be necessary to consider the safety of the child. For example, if, following a referral by a teacher, the adult caring for a child keeps her or him at home this action removes the child from the safe environment of the school in which she or he receives nurturing attention for at least part of the day. At such a time remaining at home may be particularly stressful for the child, and a child who has spoken about abuse may be punished by the parent against whom allegations have been made. Such concerns about the child's safety have to be considered seriously and a course of action agreed by professionals.

4.15 Child protection concerns often emerge in families known to one or more agencies over a long period. If professionals are working openly and honestly with the family it should be part of their approach to raise concerns about abuse with them and to invoke the child protection procedures when necessary. In such situations good supervision is important to help practitioners understand what is happening and to challenge any practice which may be detrimental to the child's safety.

Chapter 5
Immediate Protection and Planning the Investigation

Introduction

5.1 This chapter looks at the work with a family following referral. This may be action to ensure the immediate protection of the child, the provision of relevant services outside the child protection system or planning further enquiries and investigative work. It is likely that partnership will be difficult and often impossible with all family members all the time. The following paragraphs make suggestions about how professionals can ensure that families, both adults and children, can be involved as much as possible and kept informed about plans for future work.

Immediate Protection

5.2 When a referral is made the prime concern must be whether the child or children are appropriately protected. In some cases it will be necessary to verify, by an immediate visit to the place where the child is living, that she or he is safe. Most families will feel threatened and defensive when faced with professionals making a visit for this purpose. How this visit is handled can be of crucial importance to any future relationships. An open and honest approach, an unthreatening explanation of the powers and responsibilities of statutory agencies, and information for families about their rights will help to establish the beginnings of a working relationship. Parents should be encouraged to give their view of the presenting problem and any suggestions that they may have for its resolution.

5.3 In a small number of instances the removal of the child from home will be judged to be necessary. It is important at this time to assess the child's present safety and any likely deterioration in the home environment. The very fact of professional intervention may generate such distress or anger that the home becomes less safe for the child. Consideration must be given to whether an emergency protection order is required to ensure the child's safety or whether this can be properly accomplished by a voluntary agreement which establishes safe arrangements. It is important that any such agreement is adhered to by all parties, and that professionals continue to monitor the child's safety as the child protection process unfolds. The safety of the child is of paramount importance at all times.

The Need to Seek an Emergency Protection Order

5.4 When there is reasonable cause to believe that the child is likely to suffer significant harm, if she or he is not removed to alternative accommodation provided by or on behalf of the applicant, it will be necessary to seek an Emergency Protection Order. In some situations it will be necessary to seek an order on the grounds that enquiries are being frustrated because access to the child is being unreasonably refused to a person authorised to seek access. The importance of seeing and communicating with the child or young person cannot be over estimated. The reasons for this should be explained to adult carers and they should be helped to understand the responsibility of the statutory agencies to pursue allegations thoroughly. It should be possible in most cases to negotiate with the parents how seeing and communicating with the child can be achieved in a sensitive and thorough manner. How the child or young person is seen or interviewed will be determined by the nature of the allegations. For example, it will be necessary to see some children unclothed when there has been an allegation of physical abuse or neglect. In other instances, private discussions with the child will be more relevant to decision making about the validity of the allegations. On some occasions it will be useful to call upon the help of a colleague from another discipline. For example, a social worker may ask to be accompanied by a health visitor when following up allegations of neglect, or a well trusted general practitioner may be willing to visit with a social worker to win the cooperation of the family and lessen the trauma of the event.

5.5 The principles on which participatory practice and partnership are based still apply when an Emergency Protection Order is in existence. Although court action is threatening to families it will give them a positive and unequivocal message that the first priority of professionals is the protection of the child. It is essential that professionals should make explicit to families why an emergency protection order is necessary, what will happen to the child during the life of the order, how long the order will last and the possibilities for action after the order has run its course. They should be advised about their rights whilst the order is in existence, and should be given information about how to seek legal and personal support.

Children Removed from Home

5.6 If the child is removed from home, parents and carers should be encouraged whenever possible to accompany their child to the alternative place of residence whether it be the home of a relative, a hospital, a foster home or a children's home. In some instances it may be possible to find and support a member of the extended family who can care for the child in order to avoid the trauma of removal to a totally different environment. Alternatively an alleged abuser may move out of the home to avoid disruption for the child, and Section 17 of the Children Act 1989 can be used to support this course of action in the interests of the child.

5.7 Whenever possible, an alleged abuser should be encouraged to move out of the home to avoid disruption to the child. However, if a child has to be removed appropriate adults should be encouraged to accompany the child and every effort should be made to make the adults and the child welcome and comfortable on arrival at the child's new place of residence. Social workers should work closely with those receiving the child to ensure that they do not offer a cold or hostile reception to the parents, or impose unreasonable restrictions which cause further stress. Substitute carers should be encouraged to work as closely as possible with the family and be supportive to both the child and adults. Arrangements for contact should be clearly communicated to the adults in the family, the substitute carers and the children, and agreements should be reached about telephoning and receiving letters. Means of access and the need to provide or subsidise transport should be discussed. Arrangements for contact have to balance the need to enhance and strengthen family bonds at the same time as providing appropriate protection for the child. It will be important to consider whether in some cases it is inappropriate to inform the family about the child's place of residence because of the likelihood of re-abuse or threatening behaviour by the alleged abuser. In these situations families should be given information about future contact with professionals and about their involvement in decision making.

5.8 Because of the stress inherent in such situations families will not be able to absorb immediately all the information with which they are provided. Booklets giving specific advice are a positive contribution to helping parents understand what is happening and engaging them as much as possible in the process. When the families first language is not English, or when for reasons of disability use of these booklets is not possible, specific arrangements will be required to ensure that families understand what is happening, their role in the process and how they can find external support.

Allegations Which do not Require Action under the Child Protection Procedures

5.9 In contrast to cases in which immediate protection and court action are required there will be occasions when, after sharing information known to other professionals and gathering other perspectives on the allegation, the agencies with statutory powers decide that they do not need to take any action under the child protection procedures. This is a decision which should be made after careful consideration of all the information and after discussion with the appropriate manager. Some allegations will be judged to have no substance and therefore not require any further action. Alternatively it may be decided that it would not be appropriate to offer the family other kinds of service. Professionals may choose this approach hoping to work more easily in partnership with the family and avoid the stigmatising effects of child protection enquiries. Whilst this is commendable it is important that such a decision should not put a child at risk.

Planning the Enquiries and Investigations

5.10 The tasks and purpose of strategy discussions are spelt out in Working Together under the Children Act 1989 (paras 5.13.1 & 5.13.2). It is essential that a named worker co-ordinates the process of planning the further enquiries and risk assessment and takes a lead in work with the family. This worker will also have the task of collating the information and ideas of other professionals, such as doctors and health visitors, who because they know the family well can make a considerable contribution to planning at this stage. The strategy discussion must not pre-empt any subsequent child protection conference. At this point a decision should be taken whether to embark on a joint social services and police investigation or whether the social services department should pursue further enquiries themsleves and consider the possibility of providing supportive services.

5.11 Discussion about family involvement is crucial at this stage. How the family experiences the exploration of the allegations and how they are enabled to present their point of view sets the scene for any future work. Families should be consulted about the practical arrangements and they should be enabled to use their intimate knowledge of the child to assist the professionals in getting to know and understand the child.

Who should be involved in Planning

5.12 There are difficult decisions to be made about which parents and carers should be involved in helping to plan the further enquiries and investigative work, and also about how far it is safe to allow adults who have abused a child to influence these plans. A father who it is alleged has sexually abused his child may, through influencing the plans, seek to maintain control of the child or young person through fear and threats, and may persuade her or him to retract earlier statements. However, at this time the alleged abuser is likely to be expressing concern for the child and denying culpability. It is important that professionals should keep an open mind about culpability. A non-abusing parent may be able to offer considerable support to the child, and also help the professionals to conclude their task with sensitivity and the benefit of her or his understanding of the child and the alleged abuser. It is always important to assess the likelihood of collusion between an abusing parent and a non-abusing parent. At this stage much is unclear. The enquiries should be conducted as fairly as possible and above all in a manner that ensures the protection of the child.

5.13 Some situations require considerable and complex inter-agency co-operation at this stage and it may not be possible to engage the family directly in strategy discussions or even to consult them about the planning. It is important that the possibility of their involvement in future work should be considered and that all professionals should be aware of the intention to move towards more participatory practice when this becomes possible. Adults who may be suffering from Munchausen's Syndrome by Proxy or Meadow's Syndrome should not be consulted and involved at this time. Such is their deviousness that it is dangerous for professionals to make their concerns explicit before they have sufficient evidence to ensure the adequate protection of the child. It is important for the agencies with statutory responsibilities to seek expert advice before they invite such family members to engage in decision making or any level of partnership.

5.14 When the statutory agencies are planning the investigation of alleged organised abuse it is usually not possible to involve families because of the importance of maintaining the secrecy and confidentiality which is essential to the success of such an operation. However the fact that families cannot be involved in planning should not prevent professionals giving careful consideration to the interests of both adults and children and exploring ways to keep them as involved and informed as possible.

5.15 Most families will become very anxious when allegations of abuse are made, and they may feel such hostility towards the statutory agencies that they do not wish to co-operate with them. Some families may become actively obstructive. Other families or individual adults will deny that any abuse has taken place and will decline to co-operate for this reason. The fact that they do not co-operate with professionals does not of necessity mean that they are likely to harm their child. However, the likelihood of the child being harmed at this time needs careful assessment.

5.16 Topics for consideration during strategy discussions:

- the continuing safety of the child whilst further enquiries are made, for example will the child be safe as she or he is currently cared for or is there a need for protective action either on a voluntary basis or through the courts
- how parents or carers can be involved, for example who should be interviewed, what is the best place and time for interviews from the parents point of view
- whether the likelihood of an offence having been committed which will lead to a successful prosecution is such that the police should participate to safeguard evidence
- how information about children can best be gathered, for example exploring different ways of communicating with the child, whether to video or not to video, where the child should be seen and by whom should the child be interviewed, whether the child should be placed away from home temporarily
- is a medical examination needed
- when and how children should be involved, for example are they of an age and understanding to be involved, how does their current level of distress effect their involvement, should they be present at meetings or are there other ways they can contribute to decision making

- how can the views of parents or carers be given due weight when decisions are made, for example arrangements for parents to be present at meetings or are there other ways in which their views can be presented
- what practical assistance would facilitate parental involvement and co-operation, for example transport to clinics and interview suites, child care cover whilst away from home, financial assistance with transport costs or child care arrangements
- what personal support do families need, for example links with support groups, separate workers for different family members
- what arrangements should be made to facilitate the involvement and contribution of parents and children with disabilities? For example, conducting interviews in buildings with easy access, visiting disabled people at home, the use of interpreters and specialist workers who can use sign language
- whether there are issues of race, culture and language and gender that require special arrangements to be made, for example a professional worker from the same ethnic background, a worker of a specific gender, an interpreter
- whether there are members of the extended family who need to be interviewed both to provide information and as a source of support to the family, for example other siblings, grandparents, separated partners
- whether a worker known to the family should conduct the investigation or whether another worker should undertake this task, whether there is need for more than one worker
- what arrangements are needed to involve the family in pulling together all the findings and reaching a decision about further action

5.17 At the completion of the strategy discussion it is important that families are given a clear explanation of why further enquiries are necessary, how long they are likely to take, the statutory basis for intervention and the different roles of those who will have contact with the family. They also need an understanding of the possible outcomes of these enquiries.

Video Interviews with Children

5.18 During the strategy discussion it will be necessary in some cases to consider whether there should be video recorded interviews with the child which may be used in criminal proceedings, and in some instances in civil proceedings. Social workers and police officers, and other relevant professionals who know the family, must decide how far the child's involvement in criminal proceedings would be beneficial or detrimental to the particular child. Social workers have a special responsibility for safeguarding the interests of the child and representing the needs of the child to the police, and through the police to the Crown Prosecution Service (CPS). The police have a responsibility for gaining information to support criminal prosecutions. There may be considerable conflicts of purpose between the professionals and between the family and professionals. There are occasions when young people are asked to do a video recorded interview because professionals have a hunch or generalized suspicion that abuse has occurred, but there has been no allegation. Putting a young person through an interview too early, when she or he is still confused or distressed, in the hope of gaining information that could be used evidentially is unacceptable. This is not a productive or helpful experience for anyone. It is important that all decisions taken during a criminal investigation are well documented. The reasons for making or not making a video recording, and the views of individuals, should be clearly recorded.

5.19 Video recorded interviews should only be used when they are really necessary, and they should not become a routine procedure. Whether a video interview should be conducted is a matter on which the child and adult carers, as well as the different professionals, will have views. It is a matter about which they should be consulted. Children and young people should not be forced or cajoled into a video recorded interview. Once a video recording containing an allegation has been made, the child becomes technically and legally a compellable witness, even though in practice it is unlikely that a reluctant child would be compelled to give evidence. In order to enter fully into discussion carers and children need to understand the process of making the video and the possible sequence of events once it is completed. They should be made aware that they have a choice about making the video, and that if they decide not to do so there may still be a court case.

5.20 The video interview should not be allowed to dominate or eclipse other aspects of work with the family. However, it is a part of the process which causes anxiety for professionals and families, and there are clear benefits in investing sufficient time and resources in careful discussion and planning before any video recorded interviews take place. Any interviews should be conducted in accordance with the 'Memorandum of Good Practice on Video Recorded Interviews with Child Witnesses for Criminal Proceedings', and should be planned with great care so that professionals are clear about their roles and their approach, and in order to avoid additional stress on the child. They should identify any specialist advice which could help them in their task, eg a child psychiatrist, play therapist, someone with special understanding of organised abuse or institutional abuse.

5.21 Except in a small number of very urgent cases, video interviews should not be conducted immediately after a child has alleged abuse. Preparation of the child and supporting adults pays dividends in that children who are not frightened, who know what is likely to happen and are as relaxed as possible are more likely to have the confidence to talk about any abuse that has taken place. To achieve this level of confidence, they need to understand the process of interviewing and be told what will happen at different times. They must be well supported by a trusted parent, friend or professional.

5.22 The parents' knowledge of the child can be utilised to assist professionals with the decision about whether a video interview is appropriate. Parents can help professionals to assess the cognitive ability and understanding of the child, and her or his likely response to the stress of a structured video interview. Young people also have their own ideas about situations in which they are comfortable, who they would like to talk to during the interview, who they would like to support them and how they can be enabled to talk about what has happened to them. Their views should be sought and acknowledged.

5.23 Preparing the child and the supporting adult for the interview should include:

- giving a clear explanation of both the purpose and the process of the interview/s to the child and the supporting parents or carer. This should include information about their rights during the process
- discussing with both the child and supporting parents their roles during the video interviews
- planning in advance the practical details associated with the video interview. These include transport to and from the interview suite and arrangements which ensure the safety of other children in the house during the parental absence
- the acquisition at the outset, from the relevant adult and from the child, permission to interview and conduct a medical examination when necessary
- any special arrangements which would make the process easier for the child or young person. For example, a choice about the gender of the doctor conducting any medical examination
- an introduction to the team who will conduct the video interviews and other associated procedures
- discussing with the supporting parent and the child any special arrangements which should be made because of the family's race, culture or language, or because of a parent's or child's disability
- discussing what will happen to the video and any records, the need for confidentiality and who will see them
- the likely length of the interviews
- discussing what is likely to happen after the interview both in the short term and the long term, and acknowledging the difficulties of predicting future events and outcomes

5.24 Although interviews conducted according to the 'Memorandum of Good Practice' are done within an outline structure it is important that a flexible approach should be retained. Social workers have a special responsibility to safeguard the interests of the child and if any child is suffering an unacceptable level of distress the interview should be discontinued. Both the child and the supporting parent should be made aware that this is a possibility and that the welfare of the child is of paramount importance. Supervisors have a key role in helping interviewers to work in a way that is supportive to the child and avoids any abuse as a result of the process.

Monitoring Progress

5.25 Professionals can never be sure what will emerge from their enquiries. It may be necessary to replan certain tasks or seek extra information not identified as important at the outset. It may be necessary to reconsider the immediate protection of the child and possibly her or his removal from home either voluntarily or by means of a court order. Parents or carers, or maybe children, may request a change to agreed arrangements. There maybe difficulties in making changes but, if possible, requests should be accepted. If plans are re-adjusted in the light of new information, or in response to requests from professionals, it is important that families should be given appropriate details so that they understand what is happening and are party to changes of plan whenever possible.

Chapter 6
Investigation and Initial Assessment

Introduction

6.1 Some of the key messages about family participation and working in partnership which are in the two preceding chapters are repeated in this chapter. This is a deliberate repetition. Those working under the stress associated with allegations of child abuse may drift away from a working method which is sensitive to families' needs and which encourages their participation in the process. Partnership may not be possible during this stage but the principles which underpin it remain relevant.

Enquiries, Investigation and Initial Assessment

6.2 The enquiries, investigative work and the initial assessment are important steps in the child protection process both in terms of systematically gathering and evaluating information in order to assess present and future risk to the child, and also to assess the need for future work with the family. Those doing this work should make sure that families are clear about:

- the purpose of the enquiries
- the allegations to be examined
- the powers under which the work is conducted
- the rights of specific family members
- who will conduct the interviews and enquiries
- the specific roles of different professionals, for example social workers, police
- how long the enquiries are likely to take
- the possible outcomes of enquiries and investigative work, for example no further action, a child protection conference, court action, the provision of support services

Some of this ground will have been covered earlier, but families under stress often forget or do not understand clearly what they have been told. They may also have received contradictory messages from different professionals and from friends.

The Impact on Professional Workers

6.3 Child protection enquiries and investigative work can have a considerable impact on professionals. Good supervision will assist them in maintaining objectivity, evaluating information and interpreting the reactions of families, and will support them in carrying out their own role appropriately. A good supervisor will help the worker to use the skills and knowledge of other disciplines to inform their assessment of the situation. Supervision will also assist the worker to focus primarily on the child whilst at the same time working closely with the adults and involving them as much as possible.

The Possibility of Partnership

6.4 Practitioners find that the imbalance of power between the family and the professionals at this stage is such that partnership is often particularly difficult and often not possible. Sometimes the hostility and anger experienced by families precludes any possibility of partnership and even involvement. Hostility can be diminished by being clear about the tasks to be done and demonstrating a willingness to be flexible about matters that are negotiable. Families will feel more inclined to co-operate with professionals who are obviously approaching their task with an open mind rather than making assumptions and reaching conclusions on little evidence.

6.5 Partnership, and even participation and involvement may not be possible if it is thought that such an approach would give an adult the opportunity to further harm or manipulate the child. This is a difficult decision when little may be known about the alleged abuser and her or his motivation. It is the responsibility of every practitioner and supervisor to build up information and understanding about the alleged abuser. It is also important that practitioners should acquire through training and supervision an understanding of the likely behaviour of different types of abusers. A realistic and informed assessment of the risk that an alleged abuser may pose to children should underpin all decisions about parental participation.

6.6 It is important to clarify the closeness or intensity of the relationship between the primary carer and the alleged abuser. The closer the relationship the more care is required. There are occasions when the alleged abuser and the primary carer are in fact one and the same person. It may be necessary to acquire specialist advice in relation to certain cases. It is also important to explore and weigh up the protective factors in a child's environment; both the child and the adults will have valid views on this issue. On occasions young people will have strong reservations about a specific parent who has abused them being involved and interviewed. The parent, who it is alleged, has abused her or his child will also have views about what has happened and what is alleged. Such views have to be heard and weighed against other information and professional knowledge. In such situations it may be beneficial for the child and the abuser to be seen by different workers.

6.7 There are some adults who will have difficulty in contributing their ideas and views because they are physically or mentally sick or their level of distress prohibits their involvement. Some children may be too young or too disturbed to comprehend the purpose and the nature of the enquiries. It is important to give such adults and children relevant information about the process and its outcome which can be studied when the recipient is more lucid or has a better understanding of the situation. This can be particularly important for children whose lives are greatly changed by the outcome of an investigation, such as those who cease to have contact with certain family members or move to live in a substitute family.

Information for Families

6.8 When enquiries are made in relation to allegations or suspicions of abuse families should be provided with information about the child protection process. Some area child protection committees distribute copies of their procedures and others have leaflets and audio or video tapes specifically for carers and/or children. The latter have the advantage of being prepared to meet the needs of the families unlike the procedures which are designed to assist the work of professionals. Some ACPCs use material published by specialist groups such as the booklet in five languages by the Family Rights Group and the NSPCC, 'Child Protection Procedures—What They Mean for Your Family' and the publication by Parents Against Injustice 'Working in Partnership'.

6.9 Practitioners will be aware of the requirements of local ethnic groups whose first language is not English, and also the needs of those families in which carers and children have special needs because of disability. It is important that they make special arrangements either through translations, interpreters and non-written methods of communication so that these families have an understanding of the child protection process.

6.10 Families should also be supplied with information about the relevant complaints procedures. These procedures should be provided in a form easily accessible to families and they should be advised where they can turn for unbiased advice about their use. It should be made clear to all families that they have the right to complain if they are dissatisfied, and that their complaint will be dealt with as fairly and swiftly as that of any other complainant. It is particularly important that families who are accused of abuse feel that they are treated as the equals of all other complainants.

Establishing a Relationship with the Family

6.11 Even if participation and partnership are not possible at this stage the co-operation of the family is essential if the best interests of the child are to be served. Parents need to know at the outset the precise nature of the allegations against them. Thereafter it is useful to look with parents and carers, and when appropriate children, at the tasks to be covered and consider together how they can contribute to tackling each task. This approach demonstrates to family members that they are valued for their information and understanding and the unique perspective they have on the situation which is giving cause for concern. Some families refuse or are advised by friends and supporters not to co-operate. Such resistance may be dispelled if parents and carers are given a careful explanations about why enquiries and investigations are in the child's interests and why it will benefit the child if the family and professionals work with each other to reach an assessment of the situation. It may encourage some families to work more closely with professionals if they are offered an alternative social worker or a second opinion concerning the allegations.

6.12 Parents and carers should receive information about the legal background to the child protection system and about their rights. For those who do not wish to co-operate with the statutory services, it will be necessary to make explicit the powers that statutory agencies can use to protect the child in the face of hostility and non-cooperation. The possibility of seeking an emergency protection order or a child assessment order should be discussed so that the family understands the consequences of the position which they are taking.

Timing

6.13 There are time constraints under which professionals have to work. These constraints should be made explicit to families. They may not always suit individual adults and children if they prefer to build up a trusting relationship with professionals slowly. The time limits spelt out in the Children Act 1989 in relation to emergency protection orders and child assessment orders were fixed to safeguard the interests of children. A balance was struck so that the process would not be too protracted, and therefore harmful to the child, and yet allows sufficient time for the collection of relevant information to inform assessments and decisions.

6.14 The guidance in Working Together under the Children Act 1989 about the time taken to prepare material for an initial child protection conference is based on the same principle. This principle should be kept in mind when professionals are considering the possibility of extending their explorative work. There is sometimes a temptation, when trying to work in partnership, to take more time to obtain further information or see more family members. It is important to collect the relevant material to inform an initial assessment, before deciding whether to call an initial child protection conference or take some other kind of action, but it should be remembered that such delays can be stressful for families and may militate against the welfare of the child.

Who to Interview

6.15 The lead worker should see

- the child
- the care giving parent or parents of the child
- any other significant adults in the child's life
- any other children living in the household

All these people, because of their knowledge of the family's life, can make a unique contribution to the gathering and evaluation of information. Also it is likely that they will be part of any plans for the child's safety in the future.

6.16 There can be no hard and fast rules about which adults are important in a child's life. Those having the immediate care of the child, and each individual child, will have comments on the importance of various adults. It may be that adults and children will be in conflict on this issue. For example, a separated parent may minimise the value of contacting a departed partner whom the child sees as vitally important; a grandmother may be seen as interfering by a mother but a source of support by a grandchild. Professionals should seek out those who can contribute relevant information to an assessment of the situation and those who may have a role in ensuring the child's safety in the future. Confidentiality is likely to be a key issue for participants. For the sake of future relationships care must be taken not to break the trust of individuals unless it is essential for the safety of the child.

6.17 It is routine practice to see a child's mother. It should be equally standard practice to see relevant adult males, both those in the household and those living elsewhere who have parental responsibility. This is essential because they are part of the child's life and are significant either for positive or negative reasons. If professionals aspire to partnership with parents and carers it is a poor beginning to undervalue the contributions of men known to the child. Such an approach may be based on assumptions of guilt or insignificance which prove unfounded when the situation is explored properly. It may also be dangerous for the child if the worker makes only a second hand assessment of a man's potential to protect or abuse the child in the future. Additionally such action may collude with any wish the alleged abuser may have to deny involvement in the abuse.

6.18 It may be difficult for a single worker to encompass work with all the different adults and children in an extended family, either because of limited time or because of their conflicting needs. At such times co-working by two professionals can be helpful and can be a way of introducing specialist knowledge which ensures a more complete assessment. If fear of physical violence is identified as a reason why a worker is avoiding contact, then arrangements should be made to safeguard the worker either by co-working or arranging interviews in a more secure setting.

6.19 It is essential to see and when possible talk with the child. Sometimes professionals do not press for this because they fear arousing adult hostility. Fear is a shaky basis for partnership; it has to be faced and contained before partnership can be possible. Support which enables workers to tackle this fear is a key task for supervisors. If a worker cannot ask, and if necessary insist, on seeing a child then the worker is denying her or his authority and responsibilities and failing to protect the child. Children should be seen, whether or not they can communicate verbally, as an acknowledgement of their separate identity and their need for safety. It may be necessary for the worker to seek specialist help in communicating with a child who is particularly distressed or who has special needs, or if the worker personally lacks this particular skill.

6.20 If one child has been abused it is essential to consider the safety of any other children in the household. Individuals may or may not be in danger. Professionals should be straight forward and clear with adults about their need to talk with the other children both to consider their safety and to discover when appropriate their views on the current allegation. Even quite young children are often very perceptive about each other and the ways of adults, and their involvement will often provide an important perspective on the dynamics within the family.

6.21 In addition to the people whom professionals should expect to interview the parents, carers and children will have their own ideas about people who may be able to support them and offer a view on the allegation under consideration. It may be that a brother or sister of an adult carer fulfills this role, or someone who has known the family at a day centre or playgroup. A family from a particular ethnic group may wish the social worker to talk to someone who knows them well and how they function in their own group. A child may wish the worker to speak to a friend or a particular school teacher. If a child has been moved from home, the foster carer or residential worker providing day to day care will have pertinent observations to make. Whilst it is important that these contacts are followed up, the child's family may have some reservations about too many people becoming involved. These views should be respected. Some rationalisation of who can be seen will be necessary because of the time available. The guiding principle must be the need to compile sufficient information to ensure sound decision making about the protection of the child.

Where to Interview

6.22 Traditionally many interviews with parents and children are conducted in the home, some are carried out in schools and family centres and others take place in offices or special interview suites. It is important that the home should be visited but it may not be the best place for all interviews. Adults and children will have views about where they would like to be interviewed. They may prefer somewhere more neutral than their home or the worker's office, and they may feel happier if the enquiries can be conducted without oversight by neighbours.

Families should be asked about their preferences and efforts should be made to accommodate their wishes. If interviews take place away from the home it will be necessary to ensure that adequate transport is available.

6.23 Children frequently express their dislike of being interviewed at school. They may have spoken for the first time about their abuse to a teacher but it does not follow that the initial interview and enquiry should be conducted at school. Children feel that they have lost their privacy and parents feel publicly humiliated; a poor beginning for a working partnership. Over hasty interviews conducted at school tend to be a way of by-passing parents and not seeking their permission to interview.

6.24 It should be on only rare occasions that children are interviewed without the permission of their parents. It may be that a young person specifically requests an initial interview away from the home and without the knowledge of a parent. Sometimes the professionals may have sufficient evidence to suggest that both parents are implicated in the abuse and may harm or intimidate the child if they are informed of the young person's initial allegation. Only exceptionally should children be taken to a video suite and interviewed in accordance with the Memorandum of Good Practice on Video Interviewing of Children for Criminal Proceedings without prior consultation with their parents. However, it may be necessary to ensure that this prior consultation does not enable parents to put pressure on a child not to talk during the formal interview. It will only be in a case of gross sexual abuse, when both parents are implicated and there is concern for the safety of the child, that she or he should be taken to a suite without prior consultation with at least one parent. If no parent is available it will be important to find a substitute carer to provide support for the child throughout the interview.

Accommodation for Interviewing

6.25 Any facilities used for interviewing families should be comfortable and welcoming. Appropriate refreshments should be to hand. It is likely that parents and children will be seen separately as well as together and the accommodation should provide suitably equipped rooms in which those not meeting with professionals can wait in comfort and safety. If a medical examination is necessary this should be conducted in an appropriately equipped room which is comfortable and unthreatening.

Video Interview Suites

6.26 Interviews which are conducted in accordance with the Memorandum of Good Practice take place in special suites so that they can be recorded to provide evidence in court proceedings. Such suites should, in spite of the technical equipment required, be comfortable and planned to meet the needs of children and their supporters. Before any videoing takes place, the child and her or his supporter should be shown the equipment and given a clear understanding of why and how a recording is made and how and by whom their interview will be conducted. Sometimes children and their parents or carers have to travel considerable distances to reach these suites. Such journeys are stressful for families and particularly the children. Decisions have to be made, at the planning stage and throughout the process, about the value of interviewing in this way and whether the process and the ultimate court appearance will be beneficial or detrimental to the child. The parents or carers who know the child will be able to assist professionals in making these decisions.

Children Living away from Home

6.27 Some children and young people will be living in substitute care whilst enquiries and investigative interviews are carried out to assess the safety of their home. It may be appropriate to conduct some interviews with children and adults in a residential home, but the interviewing of parents in foster homes will be exceptional. During this time there should be regular contact between parents and their separated children unless a child or non-abusing parent has particularly strong reasons for wishing this not to happen. It is essential that such reservations should be respected, and supervised access may provide a compromise for some families. In some instances supervised access may be necessary to ensure that the child is protected. For example, if Munchausen's Syndrome by Proxy is suspected supervision is essential. Ultimately the safety of the child must be the deciding factor.

6.28 The purpose of any contact should be clear to all parties. Some visits should be of a social nature. Others may be planned as part of the assessment process which requires systematic observation of family interactions. The purpose of such visits should be discussed with the family and they should be aware that they are being observed. Such situations are stressful and should be kept as separate as possible from occasions when children and other family members meet to enjoy each others' company.

Allegations which are not Substantiated

6.29 After assessing the situation professionals may conclude that there is no cause for concern. At other times they may decide that, although there is some cause for concern about the welfare of the child, the likelihood of harm is not sufficient to require the calling of a child protection conference, although the family may be offered services under Part 3 of the Children Act 1989. In other cases it may be decided that there are no outstanding welfare issues which require any provision of services. Sometimes professionals may be left with uncomfortable lingering doubts and families will feel that their reputation has been sullied without any proper redress. This can be particularly painful for families if they feel that the enquiries were instigated following a malicious complaint, or if their prospects of employment have suffered as a result of the allegations. In all cases it is important that professionals should acknowledge this pain and these difficulties and give those who have been through the process the opportunity to discuss their feelings and frustrations.

6.30 Working Together under the Children Act 1989 states "The fact that the allegation is unsubstantiated may not of itself be a relief. Letters following unsubstantiated allegations should acknowledge this and the distress which has been caused". Working Together recommends that the pain of families should be recognised, not that workers should apologise for carrying out their statutory duties. If the enquiries have been handled with sensitivity, and if families have been enabled to understand the statutory process which professionals have to follow, they will be more likely to understand the spirit in which this letter is sent.

6.31 These letters are very important to many families and agencies need to be clear about whose responsibility it is to provide such a communication and what it should say. Such letters should be tailored to the needs and abilities of families to whom they are sent. Whenever possible they should exonerate families and they should always be couched in terms which encourage families to return to the social services department when help is needed. When findings have been inconclusive, it is important to seek legal advice about the wording and presentation of such communications. Many families will know from their study of ACPC procedures that the process of enquiry and assessment should be concluded in this way. It will add to their pain if a letter acknowledging their distress and summarising the outcome of the enquiries is not despatched quickly.

6.32 Sympathetic letters and explanations are not enough for many families. Counselling and support may be needed over an extended period. Some families will be unable to contemplate such help being provided by the statutory agencies and should be given information about organisations such as ParentLine, Parents Against Injustice, The Family Rights Group, Newpin and other self-help groups. If families wish to complain about the service they have received they should be reminded of the local authorities' complaints and representation procedures, and be encouraged to use them. Some families which have enjoyed the support provided by professionals during this time may feel hurt and let down if the support is suddenly withdrawn. If the social services department cannot extend support to these families they should be advised about other sources of help.

Recording Findings and Conclusions

6.33 Good practice dictates that throughout the enquiry and assessment period, and during all stages of the child protection process, workers should keep careful, clear and accurate notes of their findings and conclusions. The Access to Personal Files Act 1987 enables individuals to have access to information held about themselves on manual records. Similarly, the Data Protection Act 1984 provides for access to computer based information. Families are likely to ask for information about what is recorded about the allegations against them and the conclusions of professionals. They may wish to know where this information is held, who has access to it and for how long it will be retained. It is often difficult for them to accept that records are retained even when it has been agreed that there is no cause for concern. It is important that authorities should have a clear policy on the retention of such records and who has access to them. The content of and the rationale for this policy should be shared with families and within the limits of the law they should be given access to records about themselves.

The Initial Assessment

6.34 The outcome of enquiries, information gathering and interviews is an informed initial assessment of the level of risk to the child. The reasons for calling a child protection conference, or alternatively deciding that the allegation of abuse has not been substantiated, should emerge gradually, and both the family and the professionals should have an enhanced understanding of any problem. The report on the initial assessment should outline the findings and how they are interpreted and should be shared with the family. If there is a child protection conference, this will be the report that is presented for discussion. The contents of any such report should be known to all relevant family members including the child when appropriate. It may be necessary to safeguard certain confidential and sensitive material about particular family members.

6.35 The possibility of other kinds of action and the delivery of other kinds of services is not suspended during a child protection enquiry and investigative work. At this time it may be necessary to provide supportive services for the family to ensure that the child is adequately protected and that they are able to cope under the stress of professional scrutiny. The provision of such services should not be delayed because of an impending conference.

6.36 As more becomes known about a family it may become obvious that there is a need for protective legal action which was not recognised when only a limited amount of information was available. Family circumstances may change in a way that places the child at risk of harm. Once the need for protective action has been identified it should not be delayed either to give an opportunity for discussion of legal issues at the initial conference, or in the name of partnership. Those working with the family must take appropriate steps to ensure the immediate safety of the child even if this leads to aggravation between them and the family. It is essential to explain clearly to all concerned why such action is necessary. If court action is taken at this, or any other stage, professionals should explain to families what will happen during any court activity, and how they can find assistance to help them cope with a system which is based on an adversarial approach rather than on partnership. Such an approach is the antithesis of that which professionals will have been striving to adopt during the investigation. Families may feel undermined, or even cheated, by action which they consider to be precipitate and unreasonable. They may become hostile to professionals in a way that makes partnership in the future seem impossible. This may not in fact be the case. Honest and decisive action to protect the child may be appreciated in time and become the basis for closer co-operation and ultimately partnership.

6.37 At this time it may be decided that there are grounds for criminal proceedings at which children and adult carers will be asked to give evidence. The impact of such events should not be underestimated, and preparation for such occasions is essential. Arrangements should be made amongst professionals to keep each other and the family informed about the progress of the case and to involve relevant workers, for example members of the Crown Prosecution Service, police officers in the initial child protection conference. This is the time for early discussion with children about their involvement in the court process and it provides an opportunity to share with them the Child Witness Pack produced jointly by the Home Office, Department of Health, NSPCC and Childline.

Chapter 7
The Child Protection Conference and Decision Making About the Need for Registration

Introduction

7.1 This chapter looks at involvement and partnership during the initial child protection conference and review conferences. It assumes that professionals have tried to work as closely as possible with families during earlier contact. With strong leadership from the chair and the commitment of all professionals to be open and honest, parents can participate in conferences and assist in effective decision making. Their inclusion enables both professionals and families to be clear about the allegation of abuse, share the findings of the professionals and join in decision making about further work, including the nature and extent of partnership. Family members attending for all or part of the meeting are likely to include non-abusing carers, carers who have been involved in abuse or neglect, other adults who have a relevant contribution and children when this is appropriate. Careful decisions have to be made about whose presence will be in the interest of the child and when certain family members can be present at the same time. It will be to the benefit of families if all relevant professionals who know them well can attend in order to contribute their special knowledge and skills to the decision making.

7.2 The attendance of families at conferences and the implication for practice will need thorough discussion both within the area child protection committee and the social services department, and in all the other agencies which are represented at conferences. There should be no avoidance of the requirement for professionals to work in a much more open manner and change some of their current practice. Professionals should be provided with specific training to achieve the necessary attitudinal changes. Multi-disciplinary training should ensure that professionals move towards working in partnership in a consistent way and understand each others roles and responsibilities. Special training for those who chair conferences is essential to enable them to implement local policies which encourage families to participate in these events. They also have an important role in ensuring that all professionals can share their knowledge and expertise with families.

Preparation for Child Protection Conferences

7.3 Preparation for each conference is essential. Supervisors must ensure that workers prepare themselves and individual family members for attendance. Participants will grow in confidence and find themselves more able to contribute to successive conferences, but this will not preclude some preparation on each occasion as each event will be different.

Preparation by Professionals

7.4 Workers must know well in advance when the child protection conference or review will take place and where it will be held. They should make certain that this time is kept free from other commitments so that they can give their full attention to the meeting for as long as necessary. Those closest to the family should also set aside time for work with family members before and after the meeting. They should be in touch with the person appointed to chair the conference, and with any other relevant manager, to talk about practical difficulties in relation to the timing or the venue. In addition, they should discuss any complications which may arise during the conference because of the stance of other professionals or the need to involve a number of family members in the meeting. Dealing with any possible difficulties in advance is likely to ensure a less stressful event for families and professionals. Discussion about possible difficulties should not be conducted with the intention of pre-empting discussion that should take place at the conference.

Preparation by Managers

7.5 The person chairing a child protection conference has clear responsibilities in relation to preparation. These are dealt with later. There are other responsibilities which may, according to local management arrangements, fall to the lead social worker's supervisor, the manager who administers the conference system or the person chairing the individual conference. These include ensuring:

- that the family is aware that a conference is being held and that appropriate members have been invited
- that any exclusions of family members from the conference are agreed with the person named to make this decision, for example, a senior manager or the person chairing the conference
- that families have received all relevant information about conferences in a form which they can understand easily
- that sufficient time is set aside for each conference bearing in mind the needs of each child and adult
- that family members who have been invited receive encouragement to attend, and that as far as possible the meeting is arranged at a time convenient for them

- that all professionals who have knowledge of the family are invited to the conference
- that workers from other agencies are aware that family members will be present, and they are given the opportunity to discuss the implications of this fact with the person who will chair the conference
- that any special requirements of families are met, especially if an adult or young person has a disability or requires special facilities to aid communication
- that written reports from professionals are available at the meeting and have been shared whenever possible with the family in advance by the person preparing each report. For example, school reports, medical reports, police reports, social work reports
- that any difficulties arising from family attendance have been addressed. For example, where there are concurrent police investigations or where there are conflicts between different family members who may not be able to attend at the same time
- that an agenda is available to the person chairing each conference and all those attending the conference

7.6 These tasks have to be dealt with in advance of the child protection conference. The timescale for undertaking this work is of necessity short and therefore it is particularly important that efficient systems are in place to aid communication and sort out any problems. Families should be made aware as early as possible that they will be invited to a conference if one is called. Similarly all professionals should know that parents, carers and possibly children are likely to be at conferences and they should be ready to speak openly and honestly to the reports they have prepared for discussion.

Preparation of Families

7.7 Many family members will be unaccustomed to attending meetings, and particularly meetings in which they are the focus of attention. The contribution of adults and of children and their respective roles in the meeting will be different. Both children and adults require preparation. It is important that they should be encouraged to make as constructive a contribution as possible and should leave the meeting with a positive sense of their own worth and value rather than feeling humiliated or inadequate. Some of the inevitable stress can be alleviated if the social worker to whom the task of preparation has been allocated spends time explaining the process and discussing their worries and concerns; both with a view to making arrangements which are more suitable for the family, when this is possible, and to dispel fears based on lack of knowledge. Both children and adults can be helped to prepare information for presentation at the conference using a form of communication with which they feel personally comfortable.

7.8 It is at this time that the worker and the family should discuss which family members will attend the conference. The aims of partnerships with families must be to include parents, main carers and appropriate young people in both initial child protection conferences and child protection reviews. Paragraph 6.15 in Working Together under the Children Act states unequivocally that "exclusion should be kept to a minimum and needs to be especially justified". All area child protection committees are required to set out in their procedures criteria for such exclusions. In a small number of instances a decision will be made to exclude a particular individual for the whole of a specific conference or review on the grounds that her or his presence will be so disruptive or negative that the business of the meeting cannot be conducted. It may be decided that the presence of a particular adult may be so dangerous to the child that such a person should be excluded. If the decision is taken to exclude or limit attendance an explanation should be given for this course of action and efforts should be made to represent the persons views at the conference. Some parents or carers, even when invited and encouraged, may choose not to attend and may ask the social worker to present their views. However, experience shows that given the opportunity most wish to attend.

7.9 It may not be possible for all participants to remain in the meeting throughout the discussion. There will be conflicts of interest between participants and these may necessitate partial withdrawal from the meeting by individuals whilst specific issues are considered. Grandparents, other relatives or an estranged partner may have a contribution to make and a decision has to be made about how they should do this. Issues of confidentiality may require withdrawal by participants whilst certain information is discussed by those who need to know so that they can make sound judgements. Some young people will decline to be in the room with an alleged abuser or will be unable to speak in front of a parent or relative, but will nevertheless want the opportunity to speak with the professionals without the presence of these adults. Many adults and children will find it helpful to have a supporter at the conference, and the nature of her or his role should always be examined and clarified.

Information Required by those Attending a Conference or Review

7.10 All those invited to conferences and reviews should have clear information about:

- the name of the person chairing the conference and relevant information about her or his task
- the concerns which have led to the conference being called
- information about child protection conferences, including their legal and procedural basis
- the tasks to be accomplished and the decisions to be made
- what the consequences of the conference might be

- how the conference will be organised
- information about the definitions of abuse and criteria for registration as laid down in Working Together under the Children Act 1989
- information about the local ACPC procedures
- information about any exclusion from all or part of the conference and the reasons for this. (This information should be given in time for representations to be made about the decision.)
- who will be present and why each person will be attending
- where the conference will be held and how to travel there
- a copy of the agenda for the conference

7.11 It will help adults and children to contribute more effectively if they are assisted before the meeting to think through their own interpretation of the events which are causing concern. Also they can be helped to present their own views about how best the child can be protected in the future, including their views about the positive and negative impact on the family if the child's name is placed on the child protection register. It may be necessary to help family members rehearse how they want to put across a particularly difficult point. Some may wish to speak spontaneously and others will wish to use notes, others will want to make a written contribution or produce a tape or video recording. Sometimes it is helpful to the person chairing the conference and to other people to draw up a family tree which illustrates the complexity of family relationships and conflicts. Some families will look to the social worker for help with this task.

Pre-Conference Meeting between the Family and the Person Chairing the Conference

7.12 Experience of involving families in child protection conferences has demonstrated the value of a brief meeting before the conference between the person chairing the conference and family members. This is not to go over issues listed above, although it may be useful to check that specific steps have been taken to ease the participation of families. The purpose of the pre- conference meeting is for the person in the chair:

- to be introduced to the family
- to clarify the purpose and objectives of the conference
- to check that families have had the necessary information about the conference process
- to discuss any special needs arising from disability, language, race, religion or culture which should be accommodated at the conference
- to provide a brief description of how the conference will be conducted
- to check with family members how they would like to be introduced or if they would like to introduce themselves

- to discuss and clarify with the family the role of any supporter who is accompanying them, and meet with the supporter
- to clarify any exclusions and the reasons for these
- to ensure that the family are aware of any pending criminal proceedings and the implications of disclosure of information
- to agree a possible timescale for the conference which takes account of any constraints on the family, for example, fetching children from school
- to clarify that information shared inside a conference should not be disclosed to other people without consent.

Managing Child Protection Conferences

Setting the Scene for each Conference

7.13 There are benefits for families and professionals if there is a consistent approach to managing conferences throughout an authority. Those who attend more than once know what to expect, what is expected of them and the most useful way to make a contribution.

7.14 At the beginning of each conference all those present should be reminded of the aims and objectives of the meeting, and the reason why they are gathered together. Participants should be reminded of the confidential nature of the proceedings and that information should not be disclosed outside the conference without the permission of the person supplying that information. The person chairing the conference must protect parents against cross examination and harassment by professionals, and make sure that they are not intimidated or disadvantaged in any way. She or he must ensure that all participants keep to the stated objectives of the conference and are given the opportunity to contribute appropriately to the discussion. The conference must not stray into being a support group for professionals or a quasi-therapeutic group. The person chairing the meeting can set the tone of the occasion by spelling out for both families and professionals expectations about the use of language and the equality of opportunity for all those present.

Practical Suggestions for the Management of Conferences

7.15 There are some simple arrangements that can make it easier to manage a conference and facilitate the contribution of family members. These should be considered routinely in relation to each conference and review:

- invite the family to arrive in advance of the professionals so that they do not have to walk into a room full of strangers
- ensure, before people arrive, that there are enough chairs for those attending
- arrange comfortable waiting facilities for family members who do not remain in the meeting room throughout the conference. It may be necessary to have more than one waiting place if there is conflict within the family

The Role of the Person Chairing the Conference

7.16 The person chairing the conference has a crucial role in establishing an ethos in which openness and honesty can thrive and in which families and professionals can work together constructively for the benefit of the child. She or he should:

- make sure that all participants know the name and role of those attending. Asking people to introduce themselves and say why they are present is a useful way of beginning. It may nevertheless be helpful to have large print name cards on the table to refresh people's memory
- welcome all those attending
- stress the confidential nature of the proceedings
- remind conference members that all relevant information must be available to the conference. (If there is any information which cannot be discussed in front of any family member this should have been raised with the person chairing the conference before the meeting. However, she or he will need to be prepared for such a situation arising unexpectedly)
- make explicit at the outset what decisions and recommendations can be made, how these will be reached, and the role of different family members and professionals in this process
- give family members early opportunity to contribute to the meeting. For example, checking family details can be a good opportunity to engage families in the process
- follow an agenda which provides structure and makes the conference more focused and easier to control. It also helps all participants, including family members, understand at which point specific issues will be considered
- remind conference members to distinguish between fact and opinion, and encourage families to ask for clarification
- encourage clear, jargon-free communication and question any obscure statements
- encourage professional contributors to clarify, substantiate and justify statements made in their assessments and reports
- facilitate a debate, in which family members play a significant part, which examines the findings of reports and assessments
- summarise proceedings regularly to ensure that all those involved are aware of what is happening
- at the conclusion of the meeting summarise the decisions made, the implications of these decisions and any plans for future work. Particular attention should be paid to acknowledging the parent's or carers' contribution to the conference and to ensuring that they understand the decisions and recommendations made at the conference, and agree with professionals about the work to be undertaken after the conference
- make it clear how the proceedings have been recorded and who will receive minutes of the meeting and summaries of any action which has been agreed

An Agenda for a Child Protection Conference

7.17 The following draft agenda contains the main items which should be covered at every conference to ensure the appropriate contribution from all participants. Local ACPCs may choose to use this agenda or adapt it to meet local needs.

i) Introduction of those present
ii) Identification of key people who are absent
iii) The purpose and objectives of the conference
iv) The rules of the conference, for example confidentiality, equal opportunities
v) Verification of details about the family
vi) Presentation of the details surrounding the alleged incident or cause for concern
vii) Presentation of the initial assessment
viii) The family s perspective on the incident or cause for concern. (The child's perspective and the adult's perspective should be given separately.)
ix) Presentation of views of family members (including the feelings and wishes of the child) who are not present
x) Discussion of nature and level of risk to the child
xi) Discussion about the value of registration and its impact on the protection of the child
xii) Decision about registration
xiii) Appointment of key worker if registration is agreed
xiv) Recommendations to each agency about future action within the child protection system (an outline child protection plan) or through the provision of other services
xv) Date of the next review

7.18 If such an agenda is used it is clear to the family members that they have an important role by providing their own information and views and helping to examine the contributions of others. If no family member is present, or one or more members have not been invited, the person chairing the meeting should ensure that they are given the opportunity to make a presentation either through one of the professionals or by other appropriate means. Sometimes one family member may speak on behalf of others but it should not be assumed that one parent will necessarily represent another or that family adults can represent children. Care must always be taken to record the views of family members, including young people, and to show that they were considered at the conference.

Registration

Decisions about Registration

7.19 It is important to hear the views of children and parents about the impact of registration. The person chairing the conference must ensure that their presence does not undermine the decision making by professionals and the need to protect the child through registration when this is necessary. Some family members welcome registration whilst others see it as unnecessary and a further blow to their self esteem. Information about how each family would experience registration should be available to conference participants as it may have an impact on the effectiveness of the protection plan. The attitude of family members and their wishes about registration will be only one factor to be considered and the protection of the child must be the first priority. The person chairing the conference should remind participants that registration is only appropriate if a formal inter-agency child protection plan is needed to ensure a child's safety. Professionals, carers and when appropriate young people, should be part of, and understand, consideration of the alternatives and therefore the significance and meaning of registration. Sometimes it may be necessary to defer a decision about registration because more information is required. This delay can be very anxiety provoking for families and they should be given an explanation for the delay in reaching a decision. They should also be told as soon as possible about the date for the next conference at which registration will be reconsidered.

Action if the Child's Name is not Registered

7.20 If a decision is made that the child's name should not be entered on the child protection register, the person chairing the conference should summarise the reasons for this conclusion and ensure that the minute taker records it accurately. There should be discussion with the family about any services that may be needed and which would be welcomed by them. Any agreement to provide services should also be noted, and the task of ensuring the delivery of these services should be allocated.

7.21 Whether or not carers and children were at the conference they should receive details about the decisions made. The previous chapter outlines the work which should be undertaken with parents and children when allegations have not been substantiated and no child protection conference is called. Similar work should be carried out with each family following a conference when no registration has been made. For some the progression to the conference will have increased their trauma and feelings of resentment, and others will see the conference as a positive opportunity to put their point of view and resolve problems between them and the statutory agencies. In some instances it may assist the family to be provided with a different social worker to discuss their feelings at this stage. If there is need for extensive work, or the family have continuing support, referral to another agency may be appropriate, or a self-help group may offer advice and friendship.

Action if the Child's Name is Registered

7.22 If a decision is reached to place a child's name on the child protection register under a particular category further steps have to be taken to:

- appoint a key worker
- agree the elements of a child protection plan
- identify a group of professional workers to carry out the inter-agency work
- make recommendations to specific agencies

Family members will have their own ideas on these four matters, and their views and choices should be sought and listened to by the professionals at the conference. It may not always be possible to accommodate all their wishes and the guiding rule must be that the arrangements which are negotiated and agreed are those most likely to ensure the protection of the child.

The Appointment of a Key Worker

7.23 Family members will have views about who they would like as their key worker. Different family members may have opposing ideas. Some people will want to build on the relationship they have established in the period before the conference and others will want a complete break. Local management structures within the social services department or the NSPCC vary in how far they can accommodate such changes. The possibility of some flexibility is desirable since, for the sake of the child, it is important to nominate a worker in whom the family can feel some trust and with whom they feel they can co-operate in the future. Although there can be only one key worker, other professionals can be enlisted to do specific pieces of work and build up relationships with individual family members.

Agreeing a Child Protection Plan

7.24 At the initial child protection conference it will be possible to agree only an outline protection plan. Further assessment work will be required to establish a better understanding of the strengths and weaknesses within the family, the likelihood and sources of further risk to the child and the viability of good working relationships, and ultimately partnership, between the statutory agencies and the family. It is essential that at this stage the family understand the implications of registration and the importance of taking part in the fuller assessment of the family's strengths and problems, and the nature of harm and ways of eliminating it. It should be made clear exactly what they are being asked to contribute and what will happen if they do not work with professionals. For example, court action may become necessary if a child is not presented for assessment sessions, or if the carers do not take the protective measures agreed at the conference. The professionals for their part may need to offer assistance which facilitates co-operation by the parents, for example interviews conducted at or within easy reach of the family home and at times which suit the family.

Identifying Professionals to Work with the Family

7.25 Families whose child or children are newly registered may have a variety of needs and in many instances it will not be possible for one person to meet all of them. A group of professionals whose work is co-ordinated by the key worker should always be established. Parents and other carers should be invited to join this group unless the child is living away from home with no plans for return. Some young people may also wish to join the group. Decisions about the agencies to be involved, and the tasks each should undertake, can be agreed in principle at the initial conference, and final decisions can be reached later during discussions with parents and children and other agencies. Families may have very different views from professionals about who can help them and about the tasks which need to be done. They are often very astute in their observations about the skills and objectives of professionals and may request a different kind of help than that proposed by a group of practitioners. The objective of such negotiations must be to gather together people and a package of services which can support the family in providing adequate care for the child. There will also be tasks which require specific knowledge and skills, for example the preparation and support for a child or young person who has to act as a witness in criminal proceedings.

7.26 Professionals have a continuing role in monitoring the progress of the family and in helping them accept substitute arrangements when necessary. This may mean that the family have to accept a kind of service or a level of monitoring which they would not want if they had a totally free choice. It is important for workers to explain exactly why an alternative plan is considered to be in the child's best interests and why it is the interests of the child which must prevail in these negotiations.

Recommendations to Agencies

7.27 A child protection conference cannot make decisions on behalf of agencies but it can make recommendations for action. For example, the conference can recommend that the social services department should consider care proceedings or other court action in respect of a child. Such a recommendation may emerge as necessary following the pooling of information at a conference. The social services department will usually wish to take further legal advice on such a recommendation. It is important that families should be given a clear explanation for such action and should be helped to prepare themselves for their own appearance in court.

7.28 There is a belief amongst some professionals that court action often negates efforts to work in partnership. As stated in the first report of the Children Act Advisory Committee "the granting of a care order should not of itself impede a local authority from continuing its efforts at working in partnership with parents. The two processes are not mutually exclusive. Each has a role to play, often simultaneously, in the case management of a child at risk. Children can be placed with their families under a care order". The majority of conferences will not recommend court action but may conclude that there is a wide variety of needs within a family which could be met by the different agencies. Such recommendations should be recorded to ensure that agencies and families know what has been suggested, and what expectations they should have of each other.

Information about the Outcome of the Conference

7.29 In order that professionals and families have a clear and shared understanding about future work resulting from registration it is important that the family should be informed in writing as well as verbally of the outcome of the conference in terms of:

- the decisions and recommendations
- the outline child protection plan
- arrangements for reviews
- the name of the key worker

This information may be provided in the conferences minutes or in a summary of them or in a letter written specifically to inform families. It should be provided in the first language of the family, and in a form which suits the communication needs of relevant family members. Family members who were excluded from all or part of the conference, or who chose to stay away, will also need feedback on decisions made and future plans. Careful consideration should be given to what is appropriate information to share with each person bearing in mind the need for confidentiality, and the importance of working as closely and openly as possible with families.

Chapter 8
Comprehensive Assessment and Planning

Introduction

8.1 Following referral information will have been gathered to make an initial assessment of the child's safety and the likelihood that the child may be at risk of significant harm. Once the immediate crisis or emergency has been dealt with, and if the child's name has been registered, a more in depth assessment will be required to inform the protection plan. The purpose of comprehensive assessment is to draw together systematically information about a child and her or his family. In some instances a great deal will already be known and recorded about the family but it will be necessary to order the information and fill any gaps, in others there will be a considerable task to gather information. The purpose of collecting and analysing this material is to enable the professionals, in co-operation with the family, to weigh up their strengths and weaknesses to reach a decision about the likely future safety of the child and to consider what future action is required to ensure the child's safety.

8.2 During comprehensive assessment there are opportunities to work more closely with adult carers and to draw on their extensive understanding and knowledge of the child. There will also be more possibilities for contact with the children of the household. The earlier stages of the child protection process are usually times of pressure and stress for families and professionals because of the work to be covered within set timescales. A comprehensive assessment gives adults and children more time to build up a closer and more trusting relationship with professionals. The assessment should evaluate both in the short and the long term the possibility of working in partnership.

Comprehensive Assessment

Explaining Comprehensive Assessment to Families

8.3 Families need to know why comprehensive assessment is required and how it will be carried out. Some may have believed that with registration the scrutiny by professionals, and the need for further questions and assessment were at an end. Some may already feel so bruised that they do not wish to co- operate any longer. Adults, and children as appropriate, need to know the answers to the following questions:

- the purpose of comprehensive assessment
- who will undertake assessment work
- the timescale for assessment
- services which will be provided during comprehensive assessment
- the work to be done during assessment and what arrangements are negotiable
- who will be seen during the comprehensive assessment
- do families have to work with professionals
- what happens if families do not work with professionals
- the likely outcome of comprehensive assessment
- what families can do if they are not satisfied with the way the comprehensive assessment is carried out
- how families can complain about the assessment and the services provided

The Purpose of Comprehensive Assessment

8.4 Professionals should explain clearly to families that comprehensive assessment is required so that professionals with their assistance can make well informed decisions about the child's future protection and care. After an explanation many people will be relieved that professionals are unwilling to rush into precipitate decisions, which may involve momentous steps such as court action or removal of the child, without weighing up all the issues. For their part professionals should acknowledge that parents, members of the extended family, carers and children have useful information and valid views about the source and possible resolution of difficulties. With this reassurance that they will be given a proper hearing families are more likely to work closely with professionals. In some instances the purpose of assessment will be to collect information to inform a decision about the need for a court order. In such circumstances this should be made explicit to families and they should know that information supplied by them may be used as evidence in court. This will inevitably put limitations on working in partnership and both parties will require their own legal advice.

Who will Undertake the Work

8.5 Local arrangements for allocation of work vary and the key worker named at the initial child protection conference may or may not be the person who conducted the early enquiries and the initial assessment. The need for a change of worker should be discussed at the time of registration and family members who are present should be given an opportunity to express their preference. If family members are not present this is a matter which should be discussed with them as soon as possible. A change may undermine an embryonic partnership, or alternatively families and workers may welcome a new beginning. A unilateral decision by professionals without any discussion with or explanation to the family is no basis for close working and partnership. Whenever possible arrangements which suit both the family and professionals should be agreed.

8.6 Different family members may feel strongly that they want to see a worker of a particular gender or cultural background, or individual family members who are in conflict may ask for their own worker to help them take a full part in the assessment. Preferences should always be discussed and when possible should be accepted. If it is not feasible to accede in total to the wishes of the family, it may be possible to find the required qualities in a professional who undertakes a specific piece of work within the assessment. The role of co-ordinating the relevant contributions from the different disciplines and workers has to remain with the key worker and family members must be clear about this.

Where the Work will be Undertaken

8.7 It is important to plan with the family the venue for assessment work and to hold interviews at locations convenient for them. The family will have views about places where they feel comfortable and not threatened; and where they are free from distractions. It should not be assumed that meetings will always take place in the family home or in the offices of professionals. However, there will be occasions when a visit to a doctor's surgery or a health centre is necessary, or when professionals wish the family to attend a day centre or specialist clinic so that they can have the expert advice and observations of those working in such settings. If families are clear that these visits are necessary to make the assessment as comprehensive and thorough as possible, and if they are given assistance with travelling and other practical arrangements, they are more likely to co-operate.

The Timescale

8.8 The time required for comprehensive assessment depends on how much is already known about a family, the complexity of the family's relationships and the presenting problems. In some instances much of the information will have been collected during the initial assessment and it will be easy to clarify and build on this material. About a third of the families which pass through the child protection process are known to the relevant agencies over several years. In such cases the task is to analyse known material and clarify specific issues. It may take longer if a number of family members have special needs which have to be met so that they can contribute to the best of their ability. Some families will wish to involve a wider circle of their relations in the debate about the cause of their problems and the possible solutions. If professionals are seeking to engage families in partnership, they should be as responsive as time allows to requests for the involvement of the extended family. However, they will always be working under some time constraint. It may be that court proceedings are in hand and the court awaits an assessment report before making a decision about the child's future. Such time constraints and the reason for them should be made clear to families. Too protracted an assessment period can be detrimental to the child and confusing to adults.

8.9 It is important that comprehensive assessment should have a beginning, a programme and an outcome. It may well be necessary to deliver supportive services during this time, but it is dangerous to let work for comprehensive assessment drift on over many weeks and slide into therapeutic work. Unfocussed work endangers the child and also confuses parents and carers who may feel under endless critical observation. Such an approach undermines their confidence and their willingness to work with professionals.

8.10 One aspect of assessment is to examine whether and how far a partnership between the family and the professionals is a possibility. It should not test how far such a partnership is workable. Plans for testing the soundness of the partnership and its strength in protecting the child are made as a result of assessment and are monitored during the child protection reviews.

Who will be Interviewed

8.11 Who should be seen is a key question for discussion with the family at the beginning of assessment. Professionals will have ideas about who they want to talk to and parents, carers and children will also have views about who should be seen and who should not be seen. There may be those who were missed because they were unavailable earlier and who now need to be seen. The views of adult family members and children about who should be interviewed may be in conflict. The key worker has a professional responsibility to build up a comprehensive picture and should not collude with family members who suggest excluding people who may have crucial information and ideas.

8.12 Family members or other professionals may provide information which is highly relevant to the protection of the child but which they do not want shared with other family members or workers. Some family members are reluctant to involve relatives because they are embarrassed or ashamed and fear the disapproval of their extended family. Their dilemma should be responded to sympathetically so that they can feel supported in involving others who may have something helpful to contribute. It is important that the key worker makes it clear to both family members and other professionals that information relevant to assessment and to the protection of the child will have to be shared with those who need to know. When such information is discussed with selected people, those who provided it should be told that this is about to happen and the reason why such action is necessary. Lack of clarity and honesty on such an issue can undermine a family's willingness to work with professionals and can destroy the beginnings of a closer partnership.

Do Families have to Work with Professionals during a Comprehensive Assessment

8.13 It is to the advantage of the child if the family is fully involved in assessment, and is given every encouragement to be so. The family is a source of vital information.

In all but a very small number of cases, when the family is unlikely to have a place in the child's future life, the commitment of adults and children to plans is essential if they are to be implemented successfully.

8.14 Professionals should convey to adults and children the value they place on their contribution and should discuss with them the likelihood of a negative outcome for the child if they do not involve themselves in the assessment. Professionals should also make it clear that they wish to work co-operatively with the family. They should keep to agreements about when and how they will do things and they should always relate to the family in a non-provoking and respectful way. Both families and professionals should be clear about what arrangements are negotiable and what requirements have to be met. Professionals should be honest and explicit about the legal measures which they can take when necessary to ensure that the assessment is completed, for example, the child assessment order. They should also be clear with the family about how any lack of involvement will be reflected in the final assessment report.

The Likely Outcome of Comprehensive Assessment

8.15 Adults and children will want to know what is the likely outcome of comprehensive assessment. It must be made clear to them that its objective is to inform decisions about the child's immediate and future protection. They should be made aware that during assessment various options for action will be considered and any of these may be recommended in the final report. Families should be told that choices for action range from the child remaining at home with the support of local child protection agencies, through a voluntary agreement by which the abuser or the child moves to another place of residence, to court action which may result in a care order or a supervision order and can lead to temporary or permanent removal of the child from home or to regular statutory supervision.

8.16 The great fear for many families is court action and the removal of the child. It is important that professionals should address this matter with them without any equivocation, either to agree that it is not an appropriate option or to clarify why such action is in the child's interest. It is sometimes said that court action must be the termination of partnership. This is not of necessity true. It may be the point at which a new kind of partnership is negotiated, and the worker with statutory responsibility makes explicit her or his control in a situation which is harmful to the child. Some families are relieved when professionals take on this responsibility, and can begin to work more closely with social workers and other disciplines, either to rebuild a safe environment for the child's return or to accept the child's long term or even permanent removal. In any event court action is likely to be stressful and threatening for adult carers and children, and whatever the circumstances the key worker should ensure that the family know how to seek appropriate legal advice and personal support. Whichever of these routes is followed, there are opportunities for joint working and partnership provided families and professionals are willing to work together and are clear about their objectives.

Situations when it is Harder to Work in Partnership

8.17 During comprehensive assessment, consideration should be given to the possibilities for future work with the family and partnership with all or some family members. Research and practice experience indicate that working in partnership with certain families may be particularly difficult, risky or even impossible.

8.18 Continuing hostility towards professional intervention or total lack of motivation to be involved in planning for a child obviously precludes partnership unless these attitudes can be changed over time. A history of calculated and sadistic abuse of a child or children must raise doubts about the likelihood of partnership with the abuser unless there is unequivocal evidence of change. Persistent denial of abuse, when there is evidence that it has occurred, is not a good basis for a partnership. However, in some instances it may be possible to work with a family on a carefully structured plan to demonstrate that a child can be safe in the future. Severe and chronic mental illness, especially when it includes delusions about the child, may make negotiations impossible and undermine efforts at partnership, as may chronic substance or alcohol abuse when they dominate a parent's life.

8.19 Men who abuse their partners may also physically abuse their children. Children, whether or not they are themselves physically abused, are significantly affected by witnessing violence against their mothers. In such situations, they suffer emotional abuse by witnessing the violence and by being used by a violent man to manipulate and control his partner. Careful assessment, including specialist psychiatric advice, should be made about how far partnership is possible with a man who has persistently and sadistically abused adults and children, and how far efforts to work in this way may put children at continuing risk. If a decision is made to try to involve a violent man in the work, it is essential that the professionals should monitor carefully the dangers within the family and provide relevant services for all members of the family including the man who has been violent.

8.20 When sexual abuse has been alleged, professionals face a particularly difficult task in establishing the extent to which an alleged offender can be engaged in the work. Some practitioners hold the view that partnership is never possible because of the addictive nature of sexual abuse, the strategies which sexual abusers use to manipulate and intimidate children and partners, and because sexual abusers always minimise and deny the extent of their offending. However, other professionals take a more pragmatic view. Allegations may not be proven so that the alleged abuser remains in the household, the offender may return home after serving a sentence or the child may express a strong wish to remain in contact with the abuser once the actual abuse has been stopped. In such circumstances, some involvement by the abuser, or alleged abuser, may be necessary and possible. However, negotiating any kind of partnership will be a delicate and sensitive task depending on the nature of the allegation, the wishes of the child, the attitude and strengths of the non-abusing parent and the attitude of the abuser or alleged abuser. Much will depend on how far it is possible to work constructively with the non-abusing parent and the child. As in other situations when there are doubts about the safety of working in partnership specialist advice should be sought from those who work with abusers and can offer an assessment of the likelihood of re-abuse. It will also be necessary to assess the protective abilities of other adults in the household.

The Report on the Comprehensive Assessment

8.21 At the end of comprehensive assessment there should always be an assessment report. There are advantages in all assessment reports being prepared to a common format agreed locally by all the agencies carrying out the work on behalf of the ACPC. Such a format ensures that reports are prepared in a way that is easily accessible and comprehensible to all readers, and which can be easily adapted to another medium for readers with special needs. The report should be jargon free and as short as reasonably possible.

8.22 Primary carers, children and other adults as appropriate, should see the final report. The contents should not come as a surprise to them because of their participation in the assessment and their discussions with the key worker during the drafting of the report. However, for some the final report may contain messages which they perceive as being new or unacceptable, and they may find it difficult to agree with the recommendations. It is essential that the report should make clear the principles and knowledge which inform the views and recommendations of the professionals.

8.23 The report must spell out in precise terms the changes which must be made in relation to the adults, the child and the environment to ensure the safety of the specific child and others resident in the household. Only if families are aware of these objectives can they participate in decision making and planning.

8.24 All protection plans require resources and the assessment report should be specific about what is required from the family and also what resources should be provided by the child protection agencies or voluntary organisations to help the family achieve stated objectives. This section should be expressed in terms of what is required to make a viable plan not in terms of the ideal or what might be available. Clear and readily understandable findings, conclusions and recommendations will facilitate a thorough discussion of the report when it is presented to the family and professionals.

8.25 The assessment report will require thorough discussion by professionals and relevant family members at a meeting. This should include children if they wish to participate, have the understanding and are able to attend without undue stress. This discussion may take place at a meeting of those who have been engaged in the comprehensive assessment or at a child protection review called for the purpose. Recalling the members of the initial child protection conference has an advantage in that it engages all the agencies in the planning process and in committing resources to assist the family. On the other hand a smaller meeting is less threatening to family members, and it brings together for decision making and planning the people who will actually be working with the family. It is usually quicker and easier to assemble the smaller group and thus there is less delay before the implementation of a full protection plan properly based on a thorough assessment.

Planning

8.26 Whatever kind of meeting is used it is essential that it should be chaired and managed by an experienced and trained person. Throughout any discussion and negotiation about plans, and sometimes in the face of anger, disagreement and manipulation, the person chairing the meeting must maintain a focus on the safety of the child. Extended delay between the initial child protection conference and the agreeing of a plan may put the child at risk, and the commitment of professionals and family members may wane if the delay is unnecessarily protracted. This is less likely to occur if support services have been provided during the assessment and if all the agencies have played their full role in the assessment.

A Realistic Plan for Protection and Action

8.27 The plan for protection and action which is formulated after comprehensive assessment will have been developing since the time of referral. It will continue to develop in relation to the needs of the child and any changes within the family. It should reflect a joint approach to the problems and tasks to be tackled and the required changes, and both the professionals and the family members should be prepared to undertake specific responsibilities within agreed timescales. The details of the plan are the bench marks against which the progress of the family and the commitment of workers are measured, and therefore it is important that they should be realistic and not vague statements of good intent. It is easy when drawing up such plans to fix unachievable goals, thus re-inforcing a family's feelings of victimisation and failure. Professionals should be aware that some families wish to be seen as co-operative and therefore agree to unreasonable objectives and timescales that are too short. Setting people up to fail or allowing them to put themselves in such a position is a poor basis for closer working and partnership, and for the protection of children. It is equally damaging to establish plans which are dependent on resources which are known to be scarce or unavailable.

The Detailed Plan

8.28 Every person who has attended the meeting to discuss the assessment report should receive a copy of the detailed plan. It is often useful to have a detailed and recorded agreement signed by both professionals and family members as well as a note of the meeting. Such agreements eliminate misunderstandings and deviant interpretations about agreements and future action, and engage both the family and professionals in working positively together for the protection of the child. Working Together encourages professionals to consider the use of written agreement forms produced by the Family Rights Group and the National Foster Care Association.

Chapter 9
Implementation, Review and, when Appropriate, De-Registration

Introduction

9.1 There is a danger that, when the enquiries and assessment are complete and the child or children appear to be safe, properly focused professional interest in the welfare of the child may begin to wane. In reality, they may still be very vulnerable, and the child protection process may have undermined the confidence and skills of the adult family members. This diminution of interest is often inexplicable to families because this is the very moment at which they expect to receive additional help and support, the need for which has been identified during the earlier stages and assessment. Some families having co-operated initially with professionals begin to feel less need for working with the statutory agencies, and this view is re-inforced by any apparent reduction of professional interest.

9.2 There may be important continuing work with some families because of impending criminal proceedings at which carers and children are expecting to give evidence, and they will need support and preparation for such occasions. It is important that as well as working with family members at this time the keyworker keeps in regular touch with relevant police officers and court liaison officers, and through the police with the Crown Prosecution Service. This will enable the worker to support the family and discuss with them the development of the case.

9.3 Families and all relevant professionals should be involved in child protection reviews. Those chairing reviews should ensure the continuing involvement of all professionals who have agreed to work with the family, and also they must maintain the focus on the welfare of the child. This is the time when there can be new opportunities for working in partnership but it is also a time when professional resources may be diverted into other work.

Implementation of the Plan

The Role of Line Managers and Supervisors

9.4 Line managers and supervisors have an important role in the formulation of the plan and stopping any drift away from agreed action. Supervisors should discuss regularly with their staff the implementation of the plan, help them address any problems which arise and ensure that specific tasks are undertaken. Such discussion should include the supervisor studying the files regularly to make sure that the work is focused on agreements and contracts made and on the safety of the child.

9.5 There is an equally significant role for those who chair review conferences. It is sometimes said that these conferences are less difficult to manage than the initial child protection conference. This is not correct. There are different problems to be addressed. It is the responsibility of those chairing meetings to ensure that decisions are well founded and in the interest of each individual in the household. Each review conference requires as much commitment, careful management and preparation as the initial conference.

The Contents of the Plan

9.6 Professional workers must not delay in making an appointment to see all relevant adults and children in order to go over with them the contents of the protection plan and discuss its implementation. Delay and drift at this time gives a message that concern has diminished and that the safety of the child and partnership with the family are no longer important issues.

9.7 Partners have to be clear about their working relationships and each others expectations. It is essential that both the professional workers and relevant family members should be clear about:

- the objective of the plan, for example to provide and evaluate the efficacy of therapy, return home, alternative care
- what services will be provided by which professional group or designated agency
- the timing and nature of contact between professional workers and the family
- the purpose of services and professional contact
- specific commitments by the family, for example attendance at a family centre
- specific commitments by the professional workers, for example the provision of culturally sensitive services or special assistance for those with disabilities
- which components of the plan are negotiable in the light of experience and which are not
- what needs to change and the goals to be achieved, for example the child's weight to increase by a specific amount in a particular period, regular and appropriate stimulation for the child in keeping with her or his development and age
- what is unacceptable care of the child
- what sanctions will be used if the child is placed in renewed danger
- what preparation and support the child and adults will receive if she or he appears in court as a witness in criminal proceedings

With clarity about these matters it is possible for both professionals and the family to take issue with the other partner when their expectations are not met or when perceptions and objectives begin to differ.

9.8 Few plans move through all the expected stages. It will be necessary to renegotiate timescales and goals as it becomes evident that those agreed are not practicable, or achievable or when progress surpasses expectation. Renegotiating agreements and goals should never be left solely to the key worker. It is the responsibility of all the professionals working with the family, and the key worker should also receive advice from a well-informed supervisor. The supervisor and the key worker should consider the need to convene a child protection conference when significant changes to the plan are being considered. For example, a child may be re-injured or be persistently neglected, the key worker may change or a new adult may arrive in the household. The importance of such events must be recognised and their effect on the protection of the child examined.

9.9 There is a danger that professionals may begin to focus more on the needs of the adult carers than those of the child. This shift may occur because the worker finds it easier to relate to adults rather than to children; or it may happen because the adults caring for the child begin to demonstrate legitimate needs of their own. It is likely that at least some of these needs must be met if the child is to receive good parenting. There is a role for supervisors in making social workers aware of what is happening and enabling them to explore with the family ways of meeting the needs of both the adults and children. For example, it may be appropriate for a mother to have her own worker or to have her own time away from the pressures of family life. Alternatively, it may be necessary to see the child outside the home, and a worker in another setting may be given responsibility for talking to the child and observing her or his behaviour.

9.10 On occasions there will be a difficult decision to make between removing a child from home, or leaving her or him at home with supportive services and monitoring arrangements, which may seem to the family to be over bearing and damagingly disruptive to the normal pattern of their life. The relationships between carers and children can be undermined, rather than strengthened and supported, when the house is visited too frequently by professionals from a range of child care agencies. If a child protection plan has to be so overwhelming for those whom it is designed to help, and with whom partnership is the objective, professionals should look carefully at the level of their concern. They should weigh up the benefits of allowing a child to remain at home as opposed to an alternative plan which could include removal of the child from the home whilst therapeutic help is offered. The aim of such help would be to enable the family to care for the child in the future without the over-intrusive and disabling monitoring of professionals.

Re-injury of Children

9.11 Re-injury of children cannot be ignored. Each event should be examined thoroughly. Social workers should seek appropriate medical advice and the need for a child protection conference should be discussed with the person chairing the conference and the relevant manager. Cumulative information about injuries should be recorded and discussed with the family. It is no defence against a failure to discuss these incidents to say that such confrontation would undermine a good working relationship with the family. Most parents, even if they dislike being questioned and confronted with the facts, recognise that workers with statutory responsibilities have to deal openly and frankly with such issues, and have to discuss with them whether the child can remain safely at home or whether the abuser or child should move. To avoid raising such issues is often confusing to adults and children who see such incidents as the worker's main concern. It is also an essential component of partnership to give people the opportunity to provide their own explanation for the injury and the events which precipitated it.

Failure on Service Delivery

9.12 Sometimes the services agreed in the protection plan fail because resources cease to be available or those provided are inadequate. Such lapses or inadequacies should be acknowledged and appropriate regret expressed. To some families failure to deliver may be confusing and undermine their hopes of real help and a belief in their key worker's commitment. To others it may be the fuel for considerable anger and frustration which may eventually sabotage the protection plan and put the child at risk.

9.13 Professionals may lose sight of their original cause for concern, and services may fail or be withdrawn, without the key worker recognising the significance or cumulative effect of such changes. Routine monitoring may take the place of positive intervention, and parents may feel harassed by visits the sole purpose of which is to check that the child appears safe. Children in such situations are not always in danger of death or serious injury but they may be living very miserable and unstimulated lives with adults who feel increasingly isolated, depressed and unsupported. Good supervision which focuses on the needs of the child is essential if such situations are to be avoided and both the children and adults are to receive appropriate help.

Changes in Key Worker

9.14 Changes in key worker are a fact of life and cannot be avoided. However, they should be handled sensitively and families should be prepared for the departure of someone with whom they have established a working relationship. Continuity is important and it is valuable if the departing worker and the replacement can do some work together, or at least have a handover meeting with the family. This may be the opportunity to discuss particular attributes or skills which the family would like to see in a new worker. They may have views about the gender of the replacement worker, or may be they would like someone with an understanding of disability. People with such skills may not be readily available in large numbers and it is important that families should not be misled if the choice is limited.

New Members of a Household

9.15 Some newcomers to the household will provide positive support and some will be immediately recognisable as possibly dangerous to the child. No new arrival is insignificant. If parents and carers are working together to protect the child the family should have sufficient confidence to alert the key worker to the likelihood of any addition to the household. This is unlikely to happen in all cases, not least because some arrivals occur almost by default. For example, a new adult male may gradually move into the house. He may be a source of personal support for his female partner but he may also have a history of violent behaviour or be a Schedule I offender. The mother may not know about his violent behaviour or previous offences or she may not wish to consider their significance. It is important that, when the key worker learns of a new resident or regular visitor, she or he should discuss with the main carer the role of the new person and whether this is a threat to the safety of children in the household. If from the outset there has been clarity about the nature of acceptable care, and the sanctions which will be used when care becomes unacceptable, it will usually be possible, although often difficult and painful, to negotiate arrangements that ensure the continuing protection of the children in the household. The presence of a known offender may require that a child protection conference is convened so that the matter can be openly discussed by all professionals and relevant adults. In some instances it may be necessary for the agencies with statutory responsibilities to seek an emergency protection order if it is not possible to provide adequate protection for the children of the household by any other means.

9.16 The arrival of a new baby may be a source of harmony, or it may be a source of pressure and stress that undermines plans designed to cope with a less fraught situation. The significance of this event should be discussed with the parents and other appropriate carers and children. Views should be shared about the need to adjust the protection plan, provide a different range of services and re-think some expectations. The objective of the plan must remain the protection of all the children in the household but the means to this end may need redefining. It must be absolutely clear to family and professionals which aspects of the child protection plan have changed and how implementation should progress. It may also be necessary to consider whether a pre-birth child protection conference should be called. Such action is seen as threatening by parents, and may shake their trust in professionals, but it may be necessary to safeguard the unborn child.

Children who are Away from their Parents

9.17 Some children will have been moved from their families during the earlier stages of the child protection process and some will be moved as part of the agreed protection plan. For some it will be a voluntary arrangement and for others the separation will be enforced by a court order. In some instances it will be judged too dangerous to return a child to her or his unchanged and unchangeable home, and in some instances older children and young people, for example sexually abused teenage girls, will be clear that they do not wish to return home. Parents and responsible carers, and as appropriate children, should be involved in these decisions. However, when there is a court order the ultimate decision rests with the authority which has responsibility for implementing the order. For those children for whom return is not a possibility alternative stable arrangements must be made as speedily as possible taking into consideration their special needs and wishes. The wishes of the parents should also be taken into account provided they are not detrimental to the child. For example, parents may want a child to be placed with substitute parents who belong to a particular religious or cultural group.

9.18 When return home is a possibility the key worker, the adults and the child should be engaged in working to this end. The protection plan, in addition to laying out arrangements for current protection, should set out in detail the steps to be taken towards return. These should include the changes required and the services and support to be provided. Indicators against the possibility of return home should also be identified and monitored and recorded regularly. Efforts should be made to facilitate contact between the child and the family in terms of accommodating the child near her or his home, helping to pay travelling costs and ensuring that the family is given a warm welcome and appropriate privacy when visiting. If there is a residual fear that the child may suffer abuse at the hands of family visitors this should be discussed with them so that arrangements can be made to protect the child whilst encouraging useful family contacts.

Review

Attendance at Meetings

9.19 It is clear from the preceding paragraphs that work with families has to be constantly under review. This should be done when professionals and their supervisors meet and at meetings which include professionals and family members. Increasingly families are accepting invitations to attend child protection reviews. The review conferences usually have a lower attendance rate by professionals than initial conferences and they are therefore less threatening to all who attend. It is important that the key worker and the person chairing the meeting should ensure that all those who have commitments to the family through the protection plan attend the child protection review.

9.20 As parents and carers grow in confidence, they can make a stronger contribution and enter more easily into debate. If they have been participating between reviews in decision making they will come to reviews as more confident partners. They will have increased confidence and be able to make their own report on progress and put forward recommendations for the way forward. They should also be more able to question judgements made by professionals and propose alternative remedies to problems. These events in themselves will be of value in building confidence and those chairing reviews need to be aware of this benefit for families. The person chairing the meeting must, whilst encouraging the family's participation in the event, retain a focus on the needs of the child.

De-Registration

9.21 The primary aim of many families is to have their child's name removed from the child protection register. The guidance in Working Together under the Child Act 1989 states that de-registration is the single issue that must be considered at every review conference. The importance of achieving de-registration should not be minimised. The decision to de-register should never be a forgone conclusion, although professionals and families will have prepared together for the review and considered this decision as a possible outcome. It is an issue that should be thoroughly debated and on which the views of the family and all professionals should be heard.

9.22 Some families do not welcome de-registration because they have grown to value and depend upon professional support and they fear that this will disappear after de-registration. This view must be listened to carefully and given due credence in the debate, and so should the views of those who favour de-registration. It is the responsibility of the person chairing the conference to ensure that progress is measured objectively against the aims and targets set out in the protection plan, and that de-registration is not agreed either in a general spirit of goodwill and co-operation or in an atmosphere of indifference.

9.23 After de-registration it will be important to close this phase of work. It will be necessary to consider with the family whether any continuing help is required and whether the child should be considered as a child in need. This may be the most helpful way to proceed with families who resist de-registration because they fear the disappearance of professional support. Discussion should take place with parents and young people about whether the same workers should be involved or whether this could be an opportune time to encourage the family members to turn to another agency for assistance, or join a self-help group where they can build on strengths already established. It is particularly important to recognise the progress that a family has made and acknowledge new skills and abilities.

9.24 The summarising of work and achievements should be done verbally at the final review but it is also important to close the child protection episode with a communication to the family which confirms de-registration, recognises achievements and confirms any agreements about the delivery of services in the future. As with all earlier communications, this should be in a form which is readily accessible to all recipients and takes account of any special needs they have in relation to race, language and culture or disability. It is important that this particular working partnership is closed in as positive a manner as possible so that families feel confident about re-opening communication with professionals if and when this becomes necessary. The final child protection review may also be a good time to invite young people and adults to comment about the child protection service and how it could be improved.

Appendix 1
Team and Individual Exercises for Exploring Partnership

(These exercises were prepared by Helen Armstrong, Independent Training Consultant)

The following exercises are for use by groups of staff who normally work together and are preparing for work in partnership with families during the child protection process. The intention is that they should be used selectively when groups wish to look at particular issues as they progress and develop their approach to partnership. These exercises are no substitute for a training programme for professionals who are endeavouring to work in partnership. A companion training package to complement this practice guide was commissioned by the Department of Health from the University of East Anglia. The use of this package 'Participation in Practice—Involving Families in Child Protection', Social Work Development Unit, University of East Anglia 1992 is recommended.

Learning Activities

These activities are small-scale, and straightforward to run. They are designed for use with small groups of professionals who normally work together. The group leader in these circumstances is likely to have managerial or supervisory responsibility. The instructions for the activities give attention to this factor in facilitating the group.

The activities are aimed at expanding participants' understanding of what 'partnership' can mean and how this may apply to work with families. This means that in most activities there is not one 'correct answer' but a number of valid points which can be usefully be raised. The role of the group leader is to try to help all in the group think and share ideas on the issues raised; and to help participants relate these issues to their child protection practice.

It is necessary for the group leader to be well acquainted with the contents of this publication and confident in their knowledge and experience of local child protection procedures.

These activities are likely to be used in an everyday work setting without the formal boundaries of a training programme. Group members should be reminded that they need to consider the limits of their own sharing in the light of continuing working contacts, and the fact that the group leader may have management responsibility.

Family Feelings

Any sharing and learning around families may arouse strong feelings and divergent views. These activities do not ask participants to explore their personal experience but some do ask for contributions of ideas and feelings around families and partnership which will inevitably relate to personal experience. Group leaders need to be sensitive to individual needs and responses.

Each activity

Each activity is headed by a short section of advice on use and an outline format which gives 'at a glance' information on the shape and timing of the exercise.

In addition overall timings, a list of materials required, and detailed instructions are included for each activity.

Timings are necessarily approximate since the length of time taken by discussion depends on the numbers in the group, their confidence in discussion, the style of the facilitator, and the constraints of the occasion.

Some activities include a work sheet for photocopying or a diagram for drawing onto a flip chart or OHP.

PART 1
THE FAMILY

Activity 1 What do you think about Families?

Advice on Use

This activity is designed to focus attention on the wide range of views and experience of family life. It is important for the group leader to validate different traditions of family life.

Format

Introduce and divide into pairs; complete pair task in 10 minutes; discuss and draw out issues for 15 minutes.

Suggested timing

30 minutes.

What You Need

A flip chart to demonstrate sentences for completion.
Paper for pair working.

Activity

INTRODUCE activity.

FORM pairs and ask them to complete the following sentences in up to five different ways. Allow 10 minutes.

A family is:

....

....

....

At its best, a family can do these things for its members. A family can:

....

....

....

BRING the group together and discuss the range of ideas produced. Note variations and discuss.

RELATE the diversity in views about the family to professional experience. Widen the discussion to include the variety of family patterns encountered in work with families.

Activity 2 What do you feel about Families?

Advice on Use

The idea of 'family' can raise strong feelings. This exercise looks at how people feel about families and therefore draws upon personal feelings and experience. Group leaders should assess the possibility of personal stress for some group members.

Format

Introduce activity and divide into pairs; pairs work for 5 minutes; collect responses and discuss for 10 minutes; relate to practice and discuss for 10 minutes.

Suggested Timing

30 minutes.

What You Need

A pad of 'stickie' notes or alternative.
Flipchart for 'posting' up responses.

Activity

INTRODUCE activity giving attention to the need to set boundaries to personal sharing. Divide group into pairs.

WORDSTORM in pairs 6 words which describe participants' feelings and associations with the word 'family', writing onto 'stickies', for 5 minutes.

POOL and SHARE words. The group leader collects contributions, reads out and adds to flip chart. Discuss across whole group, sorting words into groups of similar responses for 10 minutes.

CONSIDER and DISCUSS how these different responses might impact upon practice with a family where partnership is the aim. The leader will need to give permission for doubts and concerns to be raised at this point and identify ways in which staff can obtain support when they are aware that personal factors may be affecting practice; 10 minutes.

PART 2
PARTNERSHIP

Activity 3 What is Partnership?

Advice on Use

This activity aims at assisting staff to define what partnership means in their experience. They will then be able to move on in later activities to see how this relates to the kinds of partnership they will be seeking to establish with families.

The activity draws upon personal experience directly in its use of a 'personal' category for one of the small working groups. Attention should be drawn to the need for limits on personal sharing in this area. Leaders may choose to exclude this category from the activity.

A 'working list' for partnership was developed during the four ACPC conferences organized by the Department of Health in 1992-3. The list overleaf is based upon that work. This list appears several times in these activities. It is referred to as the 'Partnership List'. At each point you may decide to use your own group's list if it covers the main areas.

Format

Introduce activity and divide into groups; small group work for 15 minutes; sharing ideas on partnership in whole group 10 minutes; draw up group 'partnership list' and compare with list below for 10 minutes.

Suggested Timing

40 minutes.

What You Need

Flip chart sheets for each working group plus large pens. It is helpful if you have drawn up the three group sheets in advance with one of the suggested pairs of headings at the top of the columns (see below).

Relationship	Partnership
What would you hope to find: In a **work** relationship (or) In a business relationship (or) In a personal relationship	**What would you hope to find:** In a **work** partnership (or) In a business partnership (or) In a personal partnership

Activity

INTRODUCE the activity. Divide into working groups, one for each topic area (work/business/personal). Give each a flip chart sheet drawn up with one set of the headings as above.

ASK each group to complete the two halves of their chart in a 'wordstorm' style session identifying what they would hope to find in a **relationship** and what they would hope to find in a **partnership** for 10 minutes.

COMPARE AND CONTRAST: each group now compares their two lists. They should aim to identify some key elements (perhaps 3 or 4) which they feel separates a **partnership** from other forms of **relationship.** 5 minutes.

SHARING ON PARTNERSHIP: across the whole group share these key elements which define a partnership. Head up a sheet **Partnership means** . . . and add your own group list of the 'vital ingredients' for a partnership in any setting for 10 minutes.

COMPARE with Partnership List below and discuss for 10 minutes.

PARTNERSHIP LIST

- shared values
- a shared task or goal
- both (or all) parties contribute resources and/or skills
- trust between the partners
- negotiation of plans
- decisions made together
- mutual confidence that each partner can and will 'deliver'
- equality or near equality between parties
- choice in entering partnership
- a formalised framework of agreed working arrangements
- open sharing of information
- mechanisms for monitoring, reviewing and ending of partnership
- dealing with power issues

Activity 4 My own Partnerships

Advice on Use

This is a **personal exercise.** It should be done by individuals **outside** the work setting. Its purpose is to reflect upon how the partnership elements identified by the group work in real life experience. This activity needs to follow Activity 3. There is no direct feedback to the group or facilitator from this activity.

Format

Individuals should work through the check list and record information entirely for their own use in their own time.

Suggested Timing

Personal choice.

What You Need

Copies of the check list for each individual together with a copy of the 'partnership list' you choose to use (you may use your own group list or that given at the end of Activity 3).

Activity

Distribute the check lists. Emphasise that the activity is a personal one and requires no feed back to the group though you may welcome comments at the start of your next session.

Partnership Check List

Personal and Confidential

Please complete the following checklist of questions. This information is entirely confidential and for your own learning and use.

You have just considered the difference between a relationship and a partnership. In the light of that discussion;

CONSIDER a partnership in your life—it may be personal or professional, now or in the past. Examples might include a partnership agreement to buy or rent property; to live together; to complete a project; to run an event etc ....

WHY was this partnership formed?

....

IS there a time limit agreed for the partnership?
YES/NO..
If so what is that limit?..

WHAT do the partners plan to get from being in this partnership? Is it the same for both (or more) partners?

....

HOW is the partnership better than doing this activity alone? What do you gain that would not be possible alone?

....

HOW will you know if the partnership is 'successful'? See if you can list up to three standards or criteria of 'success' you might want to apply to this partnership. What would 'success' look like?

....

WHAT will happen if the partnership is not successful by these standards? Will you modify your expectations, goals etc. Will you close down the partnership?

....

CAN one party close down the partnership?

....

AFTER completing this review of a personal experience of partnership, consider which areas of partnership cause you to react most strongly or have highest expectations.

FINALLY consider how your experience compares to partnership between a child protection agency and a family.

PART 3
PARTNERSHIP WITH FAMILIES

Activity 5 Partnership in Action

Advice on Use

Participants will be sharing practice and case experience to some degree. Confidentiality needs attention and the limits of confidentiality where unsafe practice may be identified.

Format

Introduce and revisit the partnership list for 5 minutes; pairs compare list to practice experience for 10 minutes; share issues for 10 minutes; discuss user perspective for 10 minutes.

Suggested Timing

40 minutes.

What You Need

A copy of the partnership list on OHP, flip chart or individual copies (you may use your own or that given in Activity 3).

Activity

INTRODUCE and remind group of the partnership list.

ASK PAIRS to relate this list to work with families now and in the past, marking which elements they think are usually present in that relationship. The two participants should help each other complete the task and note down any areas of difficulty or possible shortfalls for 10 minutes.

FEEDBACK AND DISCUSS in the whole group. Note key concerns and issues for 10 minutes.

CONSIDER THE FAMILY VIEW. Ask the group to suggest what families might think, what elements of this list might they experience as missing, or difficult to handle. Leader draws out key points for practice, identifying areas which will need attention and time in work with families for 10 minutes.

EMPHASISE that this exercise is not equivalent to asking for feedback from users of services. Checking out with users their experience of partnership could be an extension of this activity.

Activity 6 Partnership with a Child

Advice on Use

This activity allows group members to explore their views on how possible it is to have a partnership with a child, and what such a partnership might mean. The small group task requires creative thinking.

Format

Introduce the activity; small group working for 20 minutes; share and discuss for 15 minutes.

Suggested Timing

40 minutes.

What You Need

Flip charts and pens for small groups.
Copy of partnership list copied for each small group. (You may use your own or that given in Activity 3).

Activity

INTRODUCE activity and remind the group of the partnership list. Divide the group into three small working groups.

ASK each to focus on a child of a different age and 'draw' their child in the middle of their flip chart sheet. Appropriate ages are five years old; nine years old; fourteen years old. It helps to give the child a name—Darren aged 9—for example. The group can sketch in a possible family for their child. Draw up for 5 minutes.

CONSIDER in groups the different ways in which children can choose to work with professionals and think of how this child might work with your agency. Write these in around the outside of the flip chart sheet for 5 minutes.

NOW ASK each group to refer to the partnership list (you may use your own or that given in Activity 3) and consider whether 'their' child could be a 'partner' in the kind of partnership suggested? Could this child agree to the elements of partnership listed or contribute in this way? They should note comments against different elements of the list for 10 minutes.

SHARE across the whole group. Review implications for practice. 15 minutes.

Activity 7 The Personal Response

Advice on Use

This activity is designed to stimulate discussion on a number of issues which are relevant to working in partnership with families. If the discussion is going to usefully reflect experience, there needs to be a foundation of mutual trust and confidence within the group or team. At the same time it must be made clear that practice which is unsafe or contrary to policy may need follow up by management or in supervision. This activity may help identify areas which need more support or training.

Format

Introduction and pair work for 15 minutes: discussion 15 minutes.

Suggested Timing

30 minutes.

What You Need

Copies of work sheet for each pair of staff. (see next page)

Activity

INTRODUCE and ask group to work in pairs, giving each a copy of the work sheet.

PAIRS should put a mark on the line for each statement at some point between the two extremes— this mark is to indicate where they feel their views fall. If they cannot agree, ask them to put two separate marks. 10 minutes.

SHARE views and outcomes with the whole group, with attention to areas of difference and to areas of agreement. Discuss implications for practice for 15 minutes.

STATEMENTS

Partnership with a whole family just cannot work — you can only hope to form a partnership with one or two individuals.

AGREE..DISAGREE

Partnership must mean choice and families don't really have a choice about partnership in child protection!

AGREE..DISAGREE

It isn't possible to have true partnership between an agency and a child.

AGREE..DISAGREE

Sometimes men in families can be really difficult even frightening. It's better to work round them than with them.

AGREE..DISAGREE

Most parents really want the best for their children even though they may not be going the right way about it.

AGREE..DISAGREE

Activity 8 The Partnership Agency

Advice on Use

This activity poses the question—'Does your agency look like a partnership agency to families? This may lead to identification of some areas of current concern. Group leaders need to ensure that a positive target is maintained in identifying and working to overcome any perceived difficulties. This positive strategy may include following up concerns in feedback to management.

Format

Introduction; small group work for 15 minutes; sharing and discussion for 10 minutes; small group work for 5 minutes; sharing of ways ahead for 10 minutes.

Suggested Time

45 minutes.

What You Need

A flip chart and large pen for each small working group.

Activity

INTRODUCE and divide into small groups.

ASK groups to design an agency which is a **Partners' Nightmare.** Each group is working on one aspect of this agency's work with families in child protection. Ask them to list (or draw) what kinds of work they would expect from an agency which was a **non-partnership** agency (a partners' nightmare). Different groups can work on—telephone contact; home visiting; appointments at the office; planning and any other form of work or contact you wish to include. 15 minutes.

SHARE across the whole group. Compare outcomes for 10 minutes.

NOW REVERSE the picture. Ask each group to return to their nightmare scenario. Turn over the sheet and list 2-5 actions which could reverse this picture. 5 minutes.

SHARE and put up on wall as a check list for what a true Partnership Agency looks like to the user. 5 minutes.

Activity 9 Preparing for the Child Protection Conference

Limitation on Use

This activity asks for limited role play. It builds upon empathising with parents. It is an exploratory learning activity not a substitute for direct consultation of users and this should be emphasised in the introduction.

Format

Introduce the activity and set up pair interviews for 10 minutes; sharing, discussion and final outcome 20 minutes.

Suggested Timing

35 minutes.

What you will need

Worksheet for each pair drawn up into two columns as below.

Concerns/Fears	Possible Actions

Activity

INTRODUCE and DIVIDE group into pairs. Each pair represents a parent and a worker. Pairs should choose roles. The parent has been invited to a child protection conference.

SET UP AN INTERVIEW for 10 minutes with the worker asking the parent for concerns and anxieties about participation at the conference—these should be written into the left hand column of a sheet of paper. The 'worker' now asks what action could be taken to ease or allay these concerns. The pair work together to identify possible responses.

FEEDBACK to whole group and share for 10 minutes.

DRAW UP in the whole group a short list of actions which may help parents feel more confident in approaching a conference. 10 minutes.

Activity 10 Communicating in Partnership

Advice on Use

Effective communication is central to any partnership. Patterns and styles of communication will vary according to the purpose, place, and content of that communication and the relationship of those involved.

This is a simple self-monitoring activity to help raise awareness of the importance of communication and the variable effectiveness of communication in different situations. It is designed for individual completion to be followed up by sharing with a supervisor or group. Issues of effective communication will need ongoing attention in both work-place and training.

Format

Introduction 5 minutes; individual self-monitoring for a full day; 30 minute follow up with supervisor or group.

Suggested Timing

Monitoring should ideally be carried out for at least one working day. Follow-up sharing and discussion takes 20-30 minutes.

What you need

A monitoring sheet for each individual to complete for the day (see below).

Activity

INTRODUCE with emphasis on the importance of effective communication. Hand out monitoring sheets.

EACH INDIVIDUAL completes their communication monitoring sheet.
They should note occasions during the day in which they communicate with another person; decide and note down whether this communication was mainly to convey information, an opinion/judgement or feelings; note the form of communication (meeting, phone, written) and mark those that were felt to be satisfactory or successful; and those that were unsatisfactory.

REVIEW the monitoring sheet either in supervision or with a group.
Are there any conclusions that can be drawn? Have some forms of communication proved better for information?
Are these different when you want to communicate feelings or views?
Why do you think some communication was felt to be more satisfactory than others? Can you identify some factors which made them more effective?

TOGETHER try to develop three guidelines for clear communication, based on this experience. Share these with your team and use them to help you improve skills in communicating with families.

Communication Monitoring Sheet

Name..

Date of monitoring ....

Time involved:	**Time:**	**Method:** phone? meeting? written?	**Content:** information? opinions? feelings?	**Comment:** Effective or not? How and why?

PART 4
WORKING TOGETHER IN PARTNERSHIP

Activity 11 Professional Partnership

Advice on Use

Partnership with families lies at the heart of a web of other partnerships and links—those of the multi-agency child protection network. This activity is designed to raise awareness about issues of partnership with other agencies.

Format

Introduction; group working for 10 minutes; sharing and discussion for 15 minutes.

Suggested Timing

30 minutes.

What You Need

Copies of the partnership list for each participant. (You may use your own or that given in Activity 3).
List of relevant agencies on a flip chart for allocation to groups.

Activity

INTRODUCE and remind the group of the partnership list. Divide the group into small groups.

ALLOCATE to each small group, the task of looking at partnership with one other agency in the network, checking against a copy of the partnership list. Are there any shortfalls or difficulties? Are there any elements which don't apply to this kind of professional partnership? Are there additional strengths and elements you would like to identify? 10 minutes.

SHARE and compare results. The team leader asks for or makes suggestions for addressing partnership issues that have been raised. 15 minutes.

PART 5
MANAGEMENT OF PARTNERSHIP

The first two of these activities are not envisaged as group activities. They are checklists or prompts, designed to be completed individually by managers. If preferred, managers can work through the lists with a colleague of similar seniority to explore shared experience, tensions, and resources. The third activity can be utilised either in a group, a pair or individually.

Activity 12 Learning from Experience

Advice on Use

This checklist is designed for you to complete on your own or working with a colleague.

Checklist 1

1 HOW are you going to measure and record the success of working in partnership with families?

2 HOW are you going to ensure that you and other manager colleagues in the child protection network have good information on the experience of partnership as this develops?

3 HOW can you as a manager ensure that staff share their learning about the practice of partnership? How can lessons be consolidated into better practice?

4 LEARNING from experience demands a climate of work in which problems experienced at practice level are seen as opportunities for learning not as uncomfortable 'failures' to be covered up. How do you make sure that this is happening?

Possible mechanisms—which may already be in place:

- record logs identifying anxieties and problems along with positive learning outcomes;
- monthly meetings between staff team and supervisors— half hour wordstorm of problems and solutions, with positive learning experiences;
- regular report to senior management on practice experience with notes for attention;
- regular pattern of meetings between supervisors and management to check out current issues/learning points;
- workplace management groups holding short seminars on identified issues;
- a workshop on partnership experience organised through the ACPC;
- consultation with service users;
- involvement of service users in training; including the exercises in this Appendix;
- service user representation on the ACPC.

Activity 13 Learning from Experience 2

Advice on Use

This check list is for individual managers, or small groups of managers working together.

The Learning Circle

The process of learning from experience can be modelled as a circle.

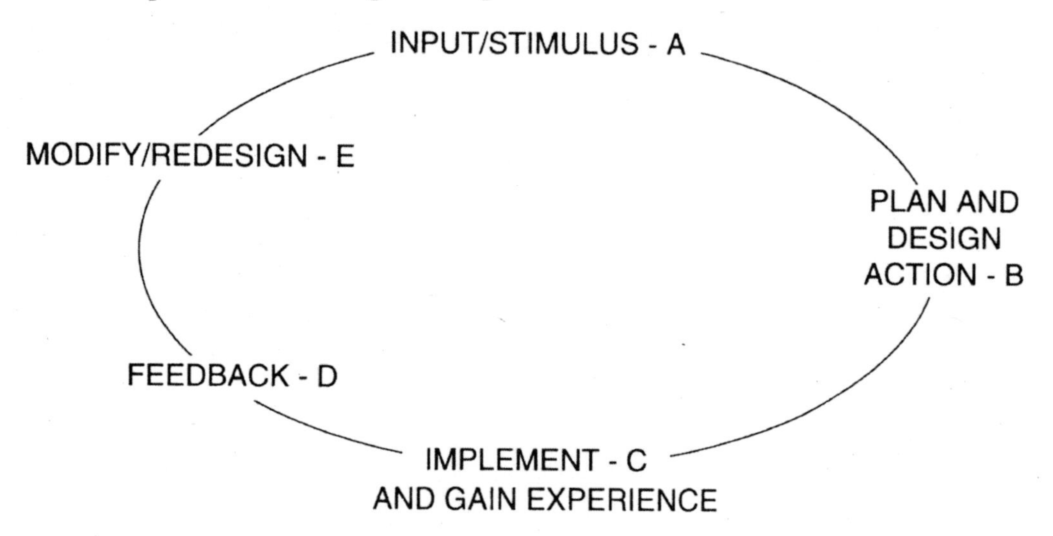

Note: each letter relates to those on diagram above.

A What training/input have your staff had on partnership with families?

B How has the practice of partnership been designed in your agency? Who decides on strategy and implementation details? Has there been the chance to share thinking with other agencies? Or in groups within your agency?

C Are staff clear about expectations on them with regard to partnership? How do they record progress and experience in this area?

D Are there clearly defined channels for feeding back staff experience through supervisors to management? How do you as a manager get information on the experience of partnership, including concerns and possible problems? Do you collate this information? Is there a forum for discussing this information and learning from it? Does the ACPC have an overview on developments?

E Who is responsible for modifying strategies and practice recommendations in the light of experience? Who agrees such changes? Is there a clear system?

A How are new ideas and approaches provided for supervisors and staff? Consider A with regard to modifications to practice?

LIST action points which arise from considering these questions and address them to your senior management or appropriate person. It may be appropriate to raise these issues at a relevant grouping of the ACPC.

Activity 14 The Partnership Agency

Advice on Use

It is vital that the implementation of the partnership approach be reviewed at the level of the 'whole organisation'.

This activity gives a format for a preliminary review of the organisation as a partnership agency. A fuller picture will require direct user consultation.

This activity can be run with a small meeting of managers, in a pair with a colleague or individually. A training colleague will be able to make useful input on current training of staff at different levels.

This activity mirrors Activity 8 which is designed in a different format for team learning.

Format

Individual completion of chart, with reference if required to colleagues or other sources of information; make out list for action and follow up.

Suggested Timing

30 minutes or as required.

What You Need

A work sheet drawn up as below.

Parent and Family	Staff involved	Training and preparation	Action: with target time

Activity

LIST into the left hand column all the methods by which a parent might contact or encounter your agency in the course of child protection ie telephone, office visit, home visit, school or hospital meeting, letter etc.

LIST ALL the people who may be involved in these encounters from reception and security staff to professional personnel.

CHECK this list. Do you know if all these people been trained or inducted into a partnership approach? What would that mean in their jobs? How confident are you that your whole agency presents a face to parents that fosters and builds partnership?

ACTION—what needs to happen to ensure that it does?

Appendix II
Additional Reading Material

1. Working Together Under the Children Act 1989 A Guide to Arrangements for Inter-agency Co-operation for the Protection of Children from Abuse (HMSO 1991 ISBN 0113214723)
2. Children Act Report 1992 (Department of Health, HMSO 1993 ISBN 0101258429)
   Children Act Report 1993 (Department of Health, HMSO 1994 ISBN 0101214421)
3. Memorandum of Good Practice on Video Recorded Interviews with Child Witnesses for Criminal Proceedings (HMSO 1992 ISBN 0113410409)
4. The Child, The Court and The Video: A Study of the Implementation of the Memorandum of Good Practice on Video Interviewing of Child Witnesses (Department of Heath Social Services Inspectorate 1994)
5. Protecting Children: A Guide for Social Workers Undertaking a Comprehensive Assessment (HMSO 1988 ISBN 0113211597)
6. The Children Act and Local Authorities: A Guide for Parents (Department of Health 1991)
7. The Children Act and the Courts: A Guide for Children and Young People (Department of Health 1991)
8. The Children Act and the Courts: A Guide for Parents (Department of Health 1991)
9. All Equal under the Children Act? (The Race Equality Unit 1991 ISBN 1873912013)
10. Child Protection Procedures—What they mean for your Family (Family Rights Group and NSPCC 1992)
11. The Child Witness Pack: Helping Children to Cope (NSPCC, Child Line, Home Office, Department of Health ISBN 0902498.52.5)
12. David Shemmings—Client Access to Records: Participation in Social Work (Avebury/Gower 1991 ISBN 1856281078)
13. Peter Marsh & Mike Fisher—Good Intentions: Developing Partnership in Social Services (Joseph Rowntree Foundation 1992 ISBN 1872470599)
14. H Giller— Children in Need: Definition, Management and Monitoring (Social Information Systems 1993 Health Publications Unit, Heywood)

Relevant Training Material

1 Participation in Practice — Involving Families in Child Protection (Department of Health and University of Anglia)

2. The Children Act 1989 — Working in Partnership with Families (Department of Health and Family Rights Group)

3. Abuse and Children with Disabilities (Department of Health and a consortium led by the NSPCC.)

4. The Children Act 1989 Child Protection Training Package (Department of Health & M Adcock, A Hollows and R White.)

Printed in the United Kingdom for HMSO
Dd 300665 5/95 C30 3400 65536 307488 47/31589